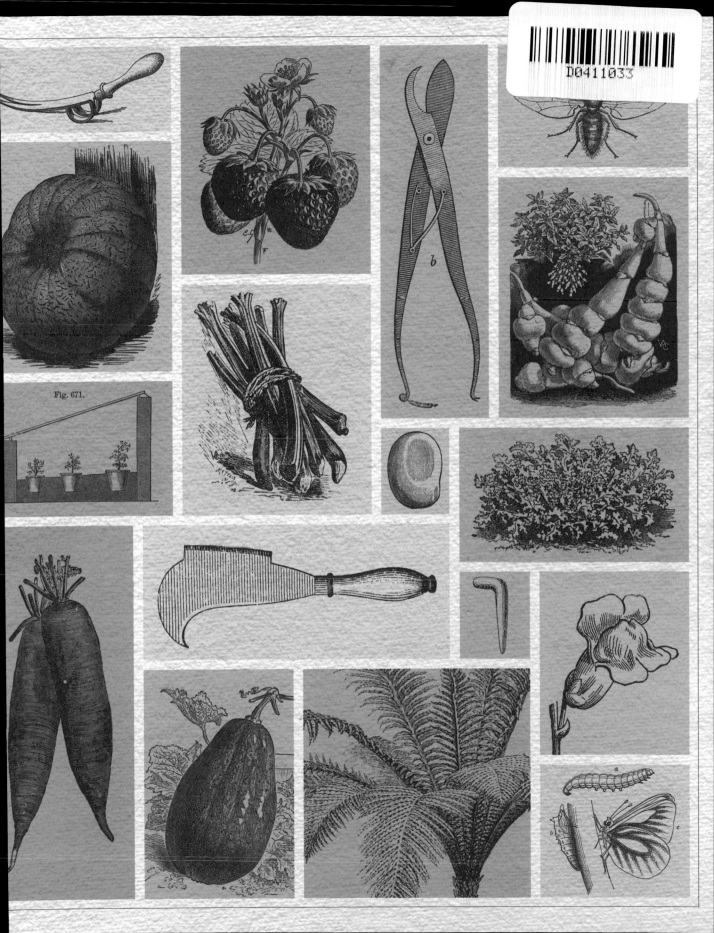

D0411033

Fig. 671.

The Kitchen Gardens at HELIGAN

The Kitchen Gardens at
HELIGAN

LOST GARDENING PRINCIPLES REDISCOVERED

Tom Petherick and Melanie Eclare

WEIDENFELD & NICOLSON

CONTENTS

INTRODUCTION

Like many before me, I started work in the garden at Heligan with precious little professional experience. In 1993, at the age of thirty-one, I had all the will in the world, terrific passion and a good training, but whatever real knowledge I possessed came from reading, watching others at work and trying a few things out for myself. The unfolding canvas that turned out to be the famous Lost Gardens of Heligan proved to be a generous provider of knowledge in those early years, for it unfolded quickly and opportunities to learn came hard and fast. For many of us, tied to the excitement and energy of the project, there was a real sense that we should have to learn quickly or we, and the restoration, would founder. For those who garden at Heligan today there is still a feeling of loyalty that has somehow been instilled by this extraordinary place, a sense that it requires a commitment beyond the ordinary: a wholeheartedness seen less and less in the modern era among manual workers, even gardeners.

LEONARD WARNE, *above*, ONE OF THE TEAM WHO KEPT THE GARDENS BEFORE THE OUTBREAK OF WAR. HE DID RETURN FROM THE TRENCHES, BUT DIED FROM INJURIES IN THE YEARS IMMEDIATELY FOLLOWING THE ARMISTICE.

This is a book about the practice of horticulture at Heligan, as it was carried out in the past and as it is now by a new generation of gardeners. Heligan, a magical garden positioned at the head of its own valley leading down to the English Channel at Megavissey, rose from the dead in the latter part of the twentieth century, its decline a direct result of having lost so many of its gardeners to the trenches of the First World War. That generation and its predecessors had kept the gardens to a very high standard. And there is little question in my mind that the popularity of the gardens today is due to the continuation of that legacy. The high standard of horticulture has been instrumental in bringing visitors in record-breaking numbers.

A hundred years ago the garden supplied the owners of Heligan House, the Tremayne family, with fresh fruit, vegetables and flowers, making it virtually self-sufficient. In the nineteenth and early twentieth centuries the walled kitchen garden was a vital part of every country estate, providing the produce of the soil. The estate farm would have eggs, meat and milk from a range of buildings grouped around the farmyard. Very often a slaughterhouse was built, standing apart from the yard. At Heligan today the farmyard has largely been turned into accommodation but some livestock has been reintroduced. The gardens, however, have assumed their previous role and now contribute to the menu offered to visitors in the popular Tea Rooms, growing the same varieties (apart from the cucumbers, the Victorian kinds being judged too bitter for modern tastes). It is a labour-intensive way of gardening and the many gardeners are friendly and approachable, their successes and failures plain for all to see. As a gardener myself I spent many hours with visitors discussing the relative merits of different methods. Sometimes the many simple, repetitious garden tasks appear to be done for their own sake, but they all contribute to the health and vitality of the garden. The damping down of the glasshouse floors on a hot day, for example, raises the level of humidity, which in turn has an effect on the breeding cycle of various pests.

Among the many strange circumstances that surround the story of the Lost Gardens of Heligan since Tim Smit and John Nelson began the restoration project in 1991, one of the most striking was the level of inexperience in the ranks of the early participants. John Nelson knew about building, and Philip McMillan Browse, who initially offered his services free as horticultural adviser, had been head of RHS Wisley and the County Horticultural Officer for Cornwall. The rest of us were

A HELIGAN STAFF PHOTOGRAPH, *below,* TAKEN BEFORE THE GREAT WAR WREAKED ITS HAVOC.

a decidedly mixed bunch, far from experienced, with many volunteers, and often with no more to our credit than great enthusiasm.

From the early 1990s the restoration slowly began to mend the devastation of decades of neglect, and now the garden is in good order, regimented in its tasks almost as if it were being run by the Victorians again. Everything not only works but works well.

I have known the garden not only as one of the original volunteers, back in the pioneering days, but later again in its ordered state. And I am reminded that there is a magical moment in the gardens when everything seems to stand still. Around ten o'clock, the gardeners have been at work for several hours, and, before the first visitor arrives, there settles on the garden an enormous sense of calm. Looking around, everything is growing in ordered rows, and there is a fresh spicy smell in the air. This is a garden at the height of its productivity, brought to that state by the work of unseen generations of gardeners.

Having toured the gardens in *Heligan: A Portrait of the Lost Gardens* and described my own connection with them, in this, its sister book, I will look at the procedures that have worked for Heligan over the last dozen or so years. It is interesting to compare today's efforts to those of our predecessors; constantly I find myself wondering whether the old-timers would have done it that way or this. We believe that our rotation system and soil fertility programme, and our reluctance to cultivate the soil using machines, are similar in thinking and practice to the methods

A TYPICAL DRAWING FROM A NINE-TEENTH CENTURY HORTICULTURAL BOOK, *above*, OF PURPLE WINTER RADISH. *Right,* ALMOST ALWAYS WRITTEN BY HEAD GARDENERS, THESE BOOKS, ARE STILL A FASCINATING AND VALUABLE SOURCE OF INFORMATION. THIS IS THE COVER OF THE HELIGAN LABOUR BOOK, WHOSE CONTENTS, *following pages*, REVEAL WHO WAS PAID HOW MUCH AND FOR WHAT TASK. THE INFLUENCE OF THE MENU IN A HOUSE SUCH AS HELIGAN WAS LEGENDARY. THE VEGETABLES NOW REMAIN THE SAME BUT THE MODES OF PREPARATION AND COOKING ARE SOMEWHAT DIFFERENT. CERTAINLY ASPIC, AS IN SALAD IN JELLY, *opposite*, WAS A GREAT FAVOUR-ITE. IT IS MUCH LESS POPULAR TODAY.

Oct 1914

NAME	MONDAY 26	TUESDAY 27
A. Smaldon.	Painting lights	Corran Eaves gutters
R. Paynter.	" "	Painting lights
J. James.	Shop	Pemppa Pump
W. Paynter.	Barn	Barn
F. Paynter.	Barn.	
J. Holman.	Estate carting	½ Estate carting ½ Gdn "
J. Trevenna	Woods.	Woods
W. H. Babe.	Cleaning	Cleaning
W. King.	Woods.	Woods
J. Rowe.	Picking fruit.	Kitchen gdn
J. Ley.	Orchard	Orchard.
J. Mills	Bothy etc	Bothy etc.
H. J. Griffin	Houses.	Houses
C. Moss.	Potting shed.	Potting shed
O. Gay.	Back door.	
A. Rundle.	Woods	Woods.

WEDNESDAY 28	THURSDAY 29	FRIDAY 30	SATURDAY 31	No. of Days	Price per day	Insurance Stamps	Amount £	s.	d.
Shop	Shop	Shop	Mansion	6	4/	3	1	4	·
...light	Barn	Painting lights	Painting lights	6	3/8	3	1	2	·
...ing	½ Absent ½ Shop	Shop	Shop	5½	3/6	3		19	3
...n	Barn	Bosue roofs	½ Bosue ½ Absent	1½	3/10	3		5	9
	"	" "	Bosue roofs	2	3/4	3		6	8
...inting	Woods	Absent	Odd carting	5	3/	3		15	·
...chard	Orchard	"	Orchard	5	3/	3		15	·
...ving	"	"	Cleaning	5	3/	3		15	·
...h	Woods	"	Woods	5	3/	3		14	2
...shoots	Orchard	"	Orchard	5	2/10	3		14	4
...hard	Border	"	Cleaning	5	2/6	4		12	6
...y etc	Botty etc	Botty etc	Botty etc	6	1/4			8	·
...se	House	House	Houses	6	3/4	3	1	·	·
...ng shed	Potting shed	Potting shed	Rock gdn	6	4/2	3	1	5	·
				6	2/10	3		17	·
				4	3/	3		12	·
...ds	Orchard	Absent	Absent			33/11	12	10	4

employed by the gardeners of about 1860, the date around which the founders of Heligan's restoration chose to model much of its horticulture.

As so much of the essence of Heligan today revolves around the type of horticulture practised in the later nineteenth century, we must consider the role of the owners of Heligan House, the Tremayne family, in the maintaining of this great garden. A family such as the Tremaynes, with many guests and a significant position in Cornish society, would have needed a sizeable amount of produce throughout the year. But there were few means of storing fresh food – ice was available only for the privileged few. If you wanted a quantity of fruit and vegetables you had to grow your own: hence the walled garden.

With large gardens came gardeners, and with great houses came servants. The relationship was crucial between the head gardener, who provided the kitchen's raw materials, and the cook, who facilitated the change from muddy carrot to exquisite soup. A further link in the chain of command was the mistress of the house. It was she, possibly with the help of the butler, the most important staff member of all, who decided what she, her family and guests and to some extent the staff were to eat.

The importance of the head gardener's role meant that within his domain his power was absolute and his knowledge was, of necessity, all-encompassing. Because sub-standard produce was unacceptable, he had a sort of divine right in dictating the means by which, at all costs, he and his staff achieved the best possible results. Those results are still sought today at Heligan, where the gardeners take enormous pride in their work – only the best is acceptable. To me the ensured success of the restoration depends upon one factor: the high standard

HELIGAN MILL, *above,* MARKS THE HALFWAY POINT BETWEEN THE GARDEN AND THE FISHING PORT OF MEVAGISSEY. WHILST THE MILL NO LONGER FUNCTIONS, THE WATER FROM A SMALL WELL IN THE BANK BY THE PATH TASTES AS SWEET AS EVER. *Right,* A SELECTION OF THE EVER BURGEONING COLLECTION OF TOOLS NOW FOUND AT HELIGAN. MANY ARE DONATIONS. SOME ARE AS APPROPRIATE NOW AS THEY WERE IN THEIR PRIME, WHILE OTHERS, SUCH AS THE DAISY REMOVER PICTURED BELOW THE SHEARS, HAVE FALLEN OUT OF FASHION AS MUCH BECAUSE OF THE ARRIVAL OF CHEMICAL CON-TROLS AS THE PAUCITY OF LABOUR.

of the horticulture instilled by Philip McMillan Browse, which has been absolutely instrumental in attracting huge numbers of visitors to the garden. This too is consistent with conditions at Heligan more than a hundred years ago, when the gardens had to be properly tended if the owner were to justify the enormous financial input required to keep them fully manned.

Today at Heligan it is hard to know precisely how the working day went in the latter part of the nineteenth century. But the gardeners continue to use many similar sorts of tools to those employed by the Victorians, and we do know how, by also following many practices from that era, what can or cannot be achieved nowadays within a given time. The sense of continuity has always been strong at Heligan and from the beginning it has played a great part in consolidating the purpose and the ideals that have brought the gardens back to life. For everyone working here who shares those ideals, it is an enduring inspiration to know that some of the results achieved today are akin to those of our truly formidable forebears.

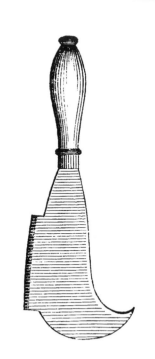

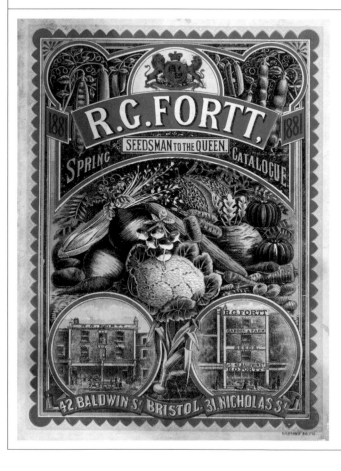

A NINETEENTH-CENTURY BILLHOOK, *above,* OF THE TYPE POSSIBLY USED TO CUT HAZEL POLES AND PEA STICKS FROM THE WOODS BELOW AND AROUND THE GARDENS, FOR USE IN THE PRODUCTIVE GARDENS. A GENERAL PURPOSE AND VERY USEFUL CUTTING TOOL, IT WOULD HAVE ALWAYS BEEN KEPT RAZOR SHARP. *Left,* THE 1881 SPRING CATALOGUE OF R. G. FORTT, BRISTOL-BASED SEEDSMAN TO THE QUEEN.

THE
PRODUCTIVE
GARDENS

1

THE LEARNING

The productive gardens are the given name for the sequence of walled gardens which make up the spine of Heligan. They comprise the Vegetable Garden, a frame yard known as the Melon Yard, a walled Flower Garden and a number of other walled enclosures including a reserve garden and a poultry yard. The decision to restore these areas as working gardens was specifically intended as a tribute to the former workforce at Heligan. It was these men who left their signatures on the walls of the thunderbox room, the old lavatory used by the workers, before departing to enlist during the First World War. Today's achievements go far beyond anything that had been envisaged at first. Over an acre of annual and perennial vegetables now flourishes where once there was a jungle of trees and bramble. A fully working Pineapple Pit dominates a Melon Yard that had seemed surely beyond help, and a splendid array of Paxtonian glasshouses overlooks a Flower Garden that was once sadly neglected and rubbish-filled but which is now fully restored, having been in full-time cultivation for more than ten years.

ADRIAN BURROWS, THE FOREMAN OF THE MAINTENANCE TEAM, WITH DAVE BULBECK (LEFT) AND BOB MITCHELL (CENTRE), REPLACING THE LIGHTS ON THE FRAME OF THE PINEAPPLE PIT, *below*. IT IS A LABOUR OF LOVE, WITHOUT WHICH THE PIT WOULD NOT BE ABLE TO FUNCTION AT ITS OPTIMUM LEVEL.

One benefit to be had from the decision to restore these gardens, taken in the early days of the overall project, was that it immediately set out a stall. In effect it declared that, 'We are going to garden this place to the best of our ability and in the manner that the Victorians did in 1860'.

Productive gardening at Heligan, carried out as it is in the same manner as in the Victorian era, provides a basis for the accumulation of an enormous amount of knowledge. The reason for this is that a very wide variety of crops are grown, from annuals through biennials, perennials and climbers, to shrubs and trees, many exactly the same as in Victorian and Edwardian times.

The passion and enthusiasm that this requires is second to none; likewise it demands from the staff an immense desire for knowledge. The catalyst for this learning has been Philip McMillan Browse who brought a lifetime of experience when he joined the project in its earliest days. As a previous holder of many senior horticultural posts, including director of RHS Wisley, he established a tradition at Heligan of learning how to practise horticulture in the proper way. By this I mean nothing has ever been left to chance. With his personal charm and an ability to give the gardeners their heads,

over the years he has allowed the garden to become a joyous place in which to work. The gardeners are encouraged to think and act for themselves and, whilst he has always been there to give advice, Philip has never interfered, preferring rather to show trust and confidence in the staff. It is the best form of management and the results are there for all to see.

All those who work in the productive gardens at Heligan have come up through the ranks. Sylvia Travers began working on fruit cultivation at Heligan after studying at Glasnevin, Dublin's Botanical Garden. She is now in overall charge of the productive gardens, an enormous responsibility to which she responds with calm thoroughness and a strongly technical approach.

As well as overseeing the Vegetable Garden, the Flower Garden

THE ICONIC PHOTOGRAPH KNOWN TO ALL SIMPLY AS 'GUNNERA MAN', *above*. THE GARDENER PROUDLY SHOWS OFF A SINGLE LEAF OF THE BRAZILIAN NATIVE *Gunnera manicata* FROM A VANTAGE POINT JUST BELOW THE PINEAPPLE PIT. THE MELON HOUSE IS IN THE BACKGROUND. THE PICTURE DATES FROM THE EARLIEST YEARS OF THE TWENTIETH CENTURY AND IS ONE OF THE MOST FAMOUS OF ALL THE IMAGES FROM HELIGAN'S PAST.

Sᴙʟᴠɪᴀ ᴛʀᴀᴠᴇʀs, ɪɴ ᴄʜᴀʀɢᴇ ᴏꜰ ᴛʜᴇ ᴘʀᴏᴅᴜᴄᴛɪᴠᴇ ɢᴀʀᴅᴇɴs, ᴡɪᴛʜ ꜰʀᴜɪᴛ ꜱᴜᴘʀᴇᴍᴏ ɢᴇᴏʀɢᴇ ɢɪʟʙᴇʀᴛ, *above*. ᴡɪᴛʜ ɢᴇᴏʀɢᴇ'ꜱ ʜᴇʟᴘ ꜱʏʟᴠɪᴀ ʜᴀꜱ ᴛᴀᴋᴇɴ ᴛʜᴇ ꜰʀᴜɪᴛ ᴀᴛ ʜᴇʟɪɢᴀɴ ᴛᴏ ɴᴇᴡ ʜᴇɪɢʜᴛꜱ ᴏꜰ ǫᴜᴀʟɪᴛʏ. *Right*, ʜᴇʟᴇɴ ᴡɪʟꜱᴏɴ ᴄᴜᴛᴛɪɴɢ ᴇᴀʀʟʏ ꜱᴇᴀꜱᴏɴ ᴅᴏʀᴏɴɪᴄᴜᴍꜱ ɪɴ ʜᴇʀ ᴅᴏᴍᴀɪɴ, ᴛʜᴇ ꜰʟᴏᴡᴇʀ ɢᴀʀᴅᴇɴ. ʜᴇʟɪɢᴀɴ'ꜱ ᴘʀᴏᴅᴜᴄᴛɪᴠᴇ ɢᴀʀᴅᴇɴɪɴɢ ʟᴇɢᴀᴄʏ ɪꜱ ɪɴ ᴛʜᴇ ʜᴀɴᴅꜱ ᴏꜰ ꜱʏʟᴠɪᴀ ᴀɴᴅ ʜᴇʟᴇɴ, ʙᴏᴛʜ ᴛʀᴀɪɴᴇᴅ ʜᴏʀᴛɪᴄᴜʟᴛᴜʀɪꜱᴛꜱ, ʙᴏᴛʜ ꜱᴋɪʟʟᴇᴅ ᴀɴᴅ ᴠᴇʀʏ ᴘᴀꜱꜱɪᴏɴᴀᴛᴇ. ᴛʜᴀᴛ ᴛʜᴇ ɢᴀʀᴅᴇɴꜱ ꜰᴜɴᴄᴛɪᴏɴ ᴛᴏ ꜱᴜᴄʜ ᴀ ʜɪɢʜ ʟᴇᴠᴇʟ ɪꜱ ᴛʜᴇɪʀ ʀᴇꜱᴘᴏɴꜱɪʙɪʟɪᴛʏ, ᴏɴᴇ ᴛᴏ ᴡʜɪᴄʜ ᴛʜᴇʏ ʀɪꜱᴇ ᴜɴꜰᴀɪʟɪɴɢʟʏ.

and the glasshouses, Sylvia still has to see to the outdoor fruit. As with fruits grown under glass, the cultivation of outdoor wall- and arch-trained fruit is a complex and time-consuming business. It is for these reasons that she must be able to have confidence that the other members of staff will carry out their work to the highest possible standards, and that they can be left alone to do so.

Mike Rundle and Charles Fleming have been at Heligan for what now seems an extraordinarily long time: Charles, who is still very much one of the lynchpins of the project, was certainly there on my first day of work in the autumn of 1993 and Mike joined soon after as another member of the Vegetable Garden's staff. Charles has always been ready and able to take on a lot of the heavy work and the weeding, and still does to this day. Their tasks through the seasons, whether they be tending the potatoes or putting in the pea sticks, are carried out with the ease of deeply ingrained habit.

Likewise Clive Mildenhall, whose previous job was as car park attendant, has also come to be an integral member of the Vegetable Garden team. Without Clive to deal with most of the winter digging there would be many sore and complaining backs.

All these people have learned a lot of their skills within the gardens at Heligan. It is worth noting that this is not done by being stood over and told how to do something; instead, each skill evolves. It is very hard to teach someone how to grade soil or double dig: they have to learn by experience and by watching others until it becomes second nature to them too.

Annie Carr and Haydn Smith have also changed departments and graduated to working in the productive gardens, Annie initially from the expanses of the estate and Haydn from the Tea Room. To watch them grow in their roles is fascinating; they are dedicated and skilled and they have had to learn it all from scratch.

Helen Wilson, who runs the Flower Garden, is another staff member who can be left alone and trusted to produce results. She has strong backup from Agnese Fornaris, a student from Italy, and staff from the pleasure grounds.

The entire productive gardens are tended as a whole by Kathy Cartwright, who joined the team soon after I left the gardens for the first time in 1996. Her all-round knowledge and love of Heligan is indispensable; it is also virtually comprehensive.

When I joined the project for the first time, Philip had already been inveigled to plan this great new venture. Now all he needed was a lieutenant. Robin Leach, the incumbent head gardener, did not express any particular interest in productive gardening and Rod Lean, who was on an industrial placement from Hadlow Horticultural College where Philip had taught, was more of a land-scape man. So it was left to me to follow my dream and grow fruit and vegetables as far as the eye could see.

Charles Fleming had already been set to work by John Nelson, growing potatoes in the Vegetable Garden. So it fell to Charles and me and various volunteers, with some help from Robin and Rod, to get started on the massive Vegetable Garden that lay in front of us. Heligan at that time was a blank canvas, and everything about it was all the more exciting.

Mike rundle, *above,* in his trademark shirt-almost-fully-undone pose, is heligan's most experienced man of the soil; a man whose knowledge of all matters agricultural and horticultural is absolute.

2 THE VEGETABLE GARDEN

Regular visitors to Heligan over the years will have noticed frequent changes to the layout and size and shape of the Vegetable Garden. The constants remain that the apple arch runs north–south down to the gate through to the Melon Yard and that the garden is laid out roughly on a cruciform grid, although there are paths which run around the outside. The box hedge that grows under the apple trees is still in good health, and the fruit grows well on the walls. Unseen, the most important changes of all happen within the soil, the basis of all healthy plant growth.

A DRAWING OF AN OPEN POLLINATED CAULIFLOWER OF THE TYPE GROWN IN THE NINETEENTH CENTURY, *above*. THE OLD VARIETIES BEAR LITTLE OR NO RESEMBLANCE TO THE TIGHT-HEADED HYBRIDS OF THE MODERN ERA AND THE TASTE HAS IMPROVED CONSIDERABLY.

THE SOIL

'Cultivation' is a word sadly lacking from our vocabularies these days, a word that we use to describe how we grow plants. It is also used in the context of the soil and how we manage it. Without the correct level of soil fertility the productive gardens would not function at the rate that we need and expect them to. So much depends on the soil, and for the plants to be in optimum health it needs to be in optimum health itself.

What a plant gets in the way of nutrition it gets from the soil. 'Feed the soil to feed the plant' is therefore the gardener's mantra. Understanding how soil functions is essential to growing healthy crops. Increasing organic matter in the soil increases the biological activity of micro-organisms by ensuring a continuous food source. It is the process of decomposition which increases the availability of nutrients, for as the organisms decompose the organic matter in the soil they help maintain good soil structure, so making the soil a more favourable place for root development. The process also helps with both drainage and water retention, allowing excess water to run off but retaining a sufficient amount to allow take-up from plant roots. The ultimate goal is a healthy, fertile, biologically active soil with improved structure and enhanced nutrient availability.

In order to preserve this precious life cycle, it is so important to feed and protect the soil, and this is why the garden is only ever cultivated by hand – rotavators are never used as their frequent use can decrease the soil's organic matter content, so in turn reducing biological activity. The Victorians had cherished the soil and a good foot of rich topsoil was found in the Vegetable Garden beneath the weeds, the decay and

MIKE RUNDLE, *below*, FOR
WHOM THE BARE SOIL OF
THE VEGETABLE GARDEN HOLDS
NO FEARS, PREPARES A SEED POTATO
FOR PLANTING, ACCOMPANIED BY
STRING LINE, BUCKET, TROWEL,
MEASURING ROD AND RADIO.

the seedling trees. The years of inactivity had not added anything in the way of fertility but the leaf fall and weed cover had offered protection from erosion. From the first day's gardening the intention was to build soil fertility to optimum levels and monitor them (organic matter cannot be built up permanently in the soil because it continues to decompose and disappears, so needs to be replenished regularly). This has been achieved and is the reason that such a diverse range of crops is able to grow so well.

In a garden such as Heligan in the nineteenth century the role of head gardener was a pivot on which all else turned. Charles McIntosh, who had worked in the gardens at Claremont for the King of the Belgians, was also the author of *The New and Improved Practical*

THE TRADITION OF PLANTING —
OR INDEED CARRYING OUT ANY
OPERATION THAT MIGHT MEAN
STANDING ON AND THEREFORE
COMPACTING THE SOIL — USING
WALKING BOARDS GOES BACK
THROUGH VICTORIAN TIMES.
ON DAMP SOIL THE BOOTPRINTS
NOT ONLY GO DEEP, THEY ARE THE
DEVIL TO REMOVE AND THEY ALSO
EFFECT A CHANGE IN THE LEVEL
OF THE SOIL. IT MAKES ALL THE
DIFFERENCE TO THE CONDITION
OF THE SOIL WHICH — AS WE HAVE
STRESSED SO MANY TIMES — NEEDS
DELICATE HANDLING, FOR IT IS THE
LIFEBLOOD OF THE GARDEN. HERE
JEREMY PEDERSEN PLANTS PARSLEY
AT A KNEEL; HE WILL FEEL IT
LATER IN THE DAY.

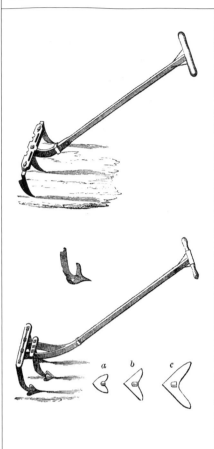

TINED CULTIVATORS, *above*, ARE STILL USED AT HELIGAN TODAY TO AERATE THE SOIL AND LOOSEN IT UP AFTER A WINTER'S WORTH OF COMPACTION FROM FEET AND RAIN. THE IMPLEMENT IS DRAGGED THROUGH THE SOIL IN THE ACTION OF A RAKE BEFORE THE SOIL IS GRADED FOR PLANTING OR SOWING. *Opposite*, PICTURES OF THE PERFECT PINERY WHICH ALSO MANAGES TO INCLUDE A HEAVY BEARING VINE. SUCH PERFECTION ONLY FOR THE VICTORIANS.

Gardener published by Thomas Kelly in 1863. In the preface to the revised edition of this marathon 973-page book he says, 'The advance which has been made in all science towards a knowledge of accurate principles, during the last few years, has been so rapid, that the arts depending upon them have attained a degree of perfection never before known. The truth of this statement may be proved by the history of any science, but by none better than that of Horticulture, in which so complete a revolution has been effected, that the works that were once considered authorities are now obsolete.' McIntosh goes on to describe the practice of horticulture as a 'delightful and useful pursuit'. Whilst it is easy to imagine the colossal pressure on a head gardener of that time to grow the finest possible produce, such a job, if McIntosh is to be believed, must also have been enthralling. In a time of unparalleled innovation, an enormous range of plant varieties were being bred (over a hundred varieties of pear are listed by McIntosh – today we struggle to find a dozen of garden worthiness); there were new types of boiler and new tools of every kind, and a revolution was taking place in glasshouse design and construction.

All these stages of development are in evidence at Heligan, where the head gardener would have overseen everything. No doubt the ever-changing practice of horticulture and the demands of an exacting employer ensure that he had to use his ingenuity and turn his own hand and the hands of his staff to anything. But, given the sufficient financial backing to be expected from a source like Heligan, the head gardener could have acted greatly to his own interest in doing the best possible job. In this, one measure of his success would be the consequent state of the soil.

Much to the advantage of the gardeners at Heligan would have been the constant availability of large quantities of horse manure, and that played a huge part in building up the soil's long-term fertility. For an estate and a garden such as Heligan it would have been provided by a number of horses that between them were kept for a variety of purposes. A pony might have pulled a plough or a harrow over small plots such as those in the Vegetable Garden, and hunters were kept by many similar households. A number of carthorses would have been put to work drawing farm machinery and wagons; and throughout the Victorian era road transport in general remained almost entirely horse-drawn. The majority of these animals were sheltered each night in stables, providing a regular source of fresh manure for hotbeds or forcing and as fermenting material for pineapple pits.

Plate V.

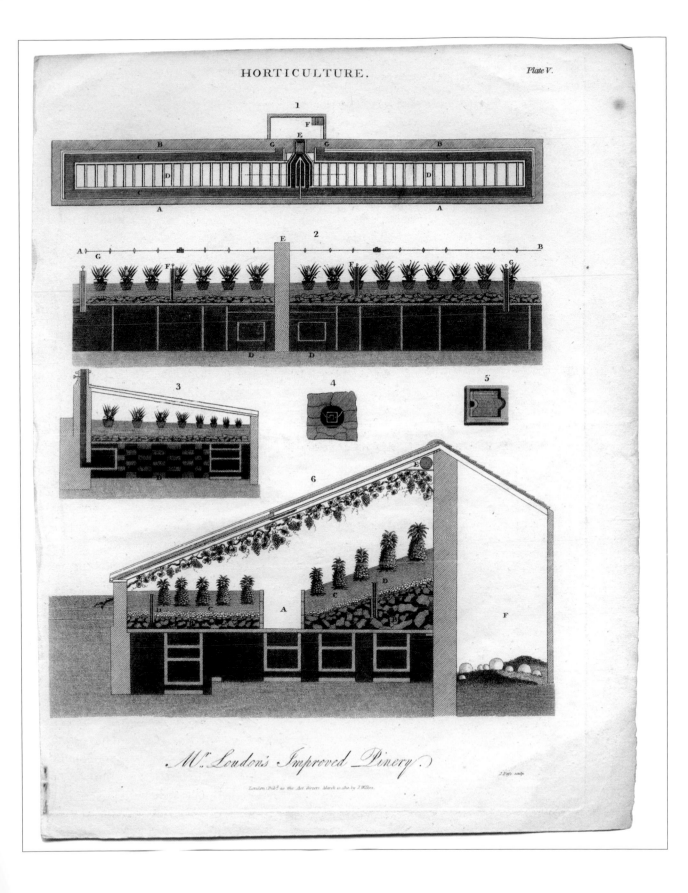

Mr. Loudon's Improved Pinery.

London: Pub.ᵈ as the Act directs. March 10.1810. by J. Wilkes.

J. Pass sculp.

A TRIANGULAR DRAW HOE OF THE TYPE COMMON IN VICTORIAN GARDENS, *below.* THE EDGES WOULD HAVE BEEN VERY SHARP AND IT IS MORE THAN LIKELY THAT THE IMPLEMENT COULD HAVE BEEN USED TO TAKE OUT SEED DRILLS. TODAY, WHILST DRAW HOES ARE STILL IN USE, THE MODERN GARDENER FINDS IT MUCH EASIER TO PUSH A FLAT DUTCH HOE RATHER THAN PULL A DRAW HOE.

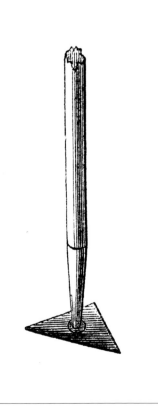

THE CROPS

The cornerstone on which success in the Vegetable Garden rests is the rotation system which in itself is a means of building soil fertility. The practice of rotating crops around land has been recognized since agriculture began and it is as relevant today as it has ever been. It breaks the life cycles of soil-borne pests and diseases and provides lasting nutrition through the use of leguminous vegetables and the addition of organic matter for specific crops during the rotation. The Vegetable Garden rotations in any one year currently number six. In order of appearance: potatoes with winter brassicas; roots; legumes; onions; cucurbits; and miscellaneous. Imagine that the majority of the garden is divided into six equal sized plots in which annual crops are grown. All six of the crops move to a different plot the next year in the order listed above. Therefore, in whichever plot the potatoes and winter brassicas are growing, when they are removed they will be replaced by the roots the following year, and this cycle will continue until six years later, when plot number one has housed all six groups of crops and will return to potatoes again.

POTATOES

Cornwall has long been famous for its potatoes. In West Penwith, in the far west of the county, early potatoes are planted at Christmas time, as demand for the first of the new season's potatoes becomes more intense with each year. The warm, relatively frost-free maritime climate provides ideal growing conditions. For early potatoes this is fine but the longer the season goes on the greater the likelihood of an attack by the dreaded 'late blight' fungus, which can have terrible consequences for the later crops of 'second earlies' and the main crops. The disease that claimed so many lives by starvation during the Irish Potato Famine in the 1840s is endemic in Cornwall. It can turn the healthiest of green potato crops into a patch of burned stumps inside a week, the crop under the ground reduced to stinking mush.

The only concession that Sylvia Travers, in running the productive gardens, makes to gardening with the use of chemicals is to spray the second earlies, main crop and salad potatoes with a systemic fungicide to prevent the ravages of the blight. She cannot afford to lose her beautiful potato crop. How could she let heritage varieties of potato, saved carefully from our own grown seed over the years, fall victim? Varieties such as Snowdrop, with a flavour of rich cream, could not be allowed to fail year after year. They would eventually die out.

SALAD RED AND SALAD BLUE, COLOURED POTATOES, *above,* WERE A POPULAR FAD WITH VICTORIAN GARDENERS. DEVOID OF FLAVOUR — FROM MY POINT OF VIEW — AND POOR COOKERS, WHAT ENDS UP IN THE POT IS GREY MUSH. NONETHELESS THE VICTORIANS WERE AVID BREEDERS AND IMPROVERS OF POTATOES AND WE MUST NOT BEGRUDGE THEM FOR TRYING. SADLY THE ONLY REDEEMING FEATURE OF THESE VARIETIES IS THEIR COLOUR IN THE RAW.

In any one season there may be as many as forty different varieties of potato grown in the garden. The majority grow in the Vegetable Garden while a selection of first early varieties are raised in the Flower Garden to take advantage of the warmer early spring temperatures found there. As with many other varieties of vegetable, the breeding of potatoes was at a peak in the third quarter of the nineteenth century. Being at the forefront of horticulture at that time it is therefore very likely that a considerable range of varieties were grown at Heligan. Today those that are grown reflect what was available towards the end of the century. They all vary in shape, size, colour (of both skin and flesh) and, in particular, flavour. Many are still in general cultivation today, such as Duke of York, Home Guard, and Sharpe's Express of the earlies, while King Edward, which is grown as both a second early and a maincrop type, is possibly one of the best-known varieties of potato in Europe.

It is important to understand that one of the main requirements that drove productive horticulture during the nineteenth century, and is still very relevant today in any form of 'kitchen gardening', was the need for successional crops, i.e. a continuous supply. As regards potatoes there are specific divisions, namely first earlies, second earlies, maincrop and salad potatoes. Each division follows on from each other with time spans of various weeks between planting and harvesting. The earlies and seconds are quick growers while the maincrop and salads require more time in the ground to 'bulk up'.

It has long been thought that maincrop potatoes were likely to have been grown on the farm at Heligan while the Vegetable Garden might have produced some of the specialist potatoes like the earlies and the salads. In light of the horrors that took place in Ireland it must have filled the Victorian gardeners at Heligan with dread at the thought of what might happen if the blight took hold in Cornwall. Without a fungicide to reach for, how did they cope? The modern organic approach is to widen row spacings to allow for the free flow of air and to cut the tops off the plants the moment there are any tell-tale signs of the disease. Today, Heligan's gardeners are careful about how they dispose of any infected tubers, and burn the infected foliage as the spores of the disease travel well and remain in the soil and compost heaps. It is my belief that the Victorians knew this and kept a very careful watch for the killer blight. The problem began in Ireland as a result of monocropping the same ground with potatoes year on year; this would not have been the case at Heligan.

The management of the potato crop has become an institution over the years. It is the reserve of three of Heligan's stalwarts, Mike Rundle, Clive Mildenhall and Charles Fleming. From planting to harvest and storage of seed to planting again it is these three who ridge and ridge the crop again, who scrape back a little soil after ninety days to take a peek at the first earlies, and who bag, store and distribute the sweet-smelling bounty. It is still done in the same manner as it would have been more than one hundred years ago, the Cornish shovel, worn from months of use, heaving soil up against the young foliage. Elsewhere this is all done by machine, but not at Heligan.

The potato crop is one that reaches the kitchens of the Tea Room almost in its entirety. Demand is high and, despite what many people imagine, the flavour of a newly dug early potato is intense. The skin has barely had time to harden off and with the addition of a little sprig of mint to the boiling water there comes a unique taste. Everyone has

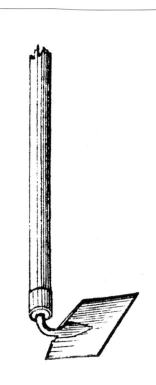

POTATO HAULM, *opposite,* A PICTURE OF HEALTH. *Above,* A DRAW HOE FOR WEEDING OR POSSIBLY RIDGING UP POTATOES. A SHOVEL IS THE CHOSEN TOOL FOR MOST FOR THIS TASK, BUT IT IS EACH TO HIS OWN.

SPRING IN THE VEGETABLE GARDEN
— AND MUCH BARE SOIL, *above*.
EARLY SUMMER BRASSICAS, TO THE
RIGHT, ARE COVERED IN NETS TO
DISCOURAGE PIGEONS AND THREE
ROWS OF ROYAL SOVEREIGN STRAW-
BERRIES ARE IN STRONG GROWTH IN
THE CENTRE. IN THE TOP SECTION
THE LEGUMES ARE IN THREE
DIFFERENT PROGRESSIVE STAGES
OF GROWTH. THE PEA 'VEITCH'S
WESTERN EXPRESS' HAS HAZEL
STICKS ALREADY IN POSITION WHICH
ARE TIED IN WITH STRING TO WIRES
HELD IN PLACE BY POLES DRIVEN
INTO THE GROUND.

their favourites but many look no further than Duke of York, an early which is waxy in its youth, becoming ever more floury with age.

Planting time for the early potatoes begins on or a few days past 1 March. Every inch of the potato patch has been trench dug through the winter and well-rotted manure, mostly spent, from the Pineapple Pit, has been incorporated. The planters inch their way along the planting boards, digging a series of individual holes three feet apart, one for each seed tuber. As they do so, it is good to know that the potatoes will be lying on what amounts to a layer of fertilizer.

Curiously, the Victorians were of the opinion that if the garden soil was considered in good enough 'heart' they need not bother to incorporate any organic matter for the first earlies. These, they felt, would not reach sufficient maturity to make this procedure worthwhile. It also meant that if they had a high enough opinion of their topsoil, the option was there.

If the March weather brings enough warmth the first sprouts will nudge their way through the soil surface after two to three weeks. It is at this point that they are at their most vulnerable. Not from blight or slugs but from the meanest killer of them all – frost. One freezing night will turn the shoots brown and crispy, but from this the plants will

Potato Snow

Ingredients:
6 potatoes for 3 persons.
Salt and water.

Mode: Choose large white potatoes, as free from spots as possible; boil them in their skins in salt and water until perfectly tender, for ½ to ¾ hour; drain and dry them thoroughly by the side of the fire, and peel them. In a hot dish before the fire, rub the potatoes through a coarse sieve on to this dish; do not touch them afterwards; or the flakes will fall, and serve as hot as possible.

IF EVER THERE WAS A PLACE TO LEARN ABOUT FLAVOUR AMONGST POTATO VARIETIES IT IS HELIGAN. THERE ARE THE GOOD, THE BAD AND THE INDIFFERENT BUT THERE ARE NO TWO ALIKE AND THERE ARE SOME REALLY GOOD ONES IN THE COLLECTION. THE MOST IMPORTANT THING TO LEARN IS THEIR LEVEL OF MOISTURE CONTENT BECAUSE THIS DETERMINES HOW THEY ARE BEST COOKED. IT IS NO GOOD TRYING TO ROAST A WAXY VARIETY, FOR EXAMPLE; THEY REMAIN SLIMY. A FLOURY ONE, ON THE OTHER HAND, WILL BE CRISP ON THE OUTSIDE, SNOWY ON THE INSIDE.

recover; two to three nights of frost in a row and they will suffer severe damage, leading to crop failure. In most years all will be well. But just occasionally yields can be badly affected if high pressure dominates the weather systems, because it is this which brings clear skies at night and with it the frost.

To combat the hazards brought on by frost the rows of young potatoes are ridged up. This is a simple process by which the soil on either side of the row is nudged up against the plants, thereby leaving as little leaf as possible exposed during the early stages of growth. As well as protecting from frost, the practice of ridging deals a deathly blow to any weed seedlings. The ridging is done by hand, with a shovel, and is carried out for a second time about a fortnight later when more leaf is showing. The ridge also acts as an underground space into which the swelling tubers can grow.

From about the seventy-day stage flowers begin to appear and it is at this point that the crop is nearing maturity. Lifting will begin at any time around ninety days, when the specially designed flat-tined potato fork has one of its few outings of the year. The potatoes will be stored ready for distribution, in paper sacks which once upon a time would have been hessian but are now made of heavy-duty paper. In the meantime suitable seed potatoes for next year's crop are set aside and laid out in wooden trays.

It is an enormous luxury to have as many varieties of potato as Heligan can boast. From ping-pong-ball size in June to late maincrop giants such as Golden Wonder (the crisping variety) and in September the sublime yellow waxiness of Pink Fir Apple, there is a flavour and a texture to suit every preference.

THE CABBAGE TRIBE

Amidst all the activity of lifting the early potatoes there runs the thread of continuity that makes the practice of horticulture such an enormously pleasurable pastime. For it is about this time that Sylvia, and Kathy Cartwright, whose work is so important to the Vegetable Garden, will think about sowing the first winter greens – the early purple and white sprouting broccolis.

'Greens' evoke mixed reactions; they tend to be either loved or loathed. Brussels sprouts are the most hated of the lot. For a gardener it is something similar. Without exception brassicas, as we should call them, are easy to germinate and a joy to grow on. Once they are in the

THERE IS NO AROMA LIKE THAT OF A FRESHLY HARVESTED HANDFUL OF NEW POTATOES, *right*. THE SQUEAK THAT EMANATES FROM THEM WHEN THEY RUB TOGETHER IS ALMOST ANIMAL AND THEY ARE THE MOST PERFECT PRODUCT TO APPEAR FROM BENEATH HELIGAN'S RICH SOIL. MIKE'S HANDS SHOW THEM WITH RESPECT AND TENDERNESS. THESE ARE THE FIRST OF THE NEW SEASON'S ARRIVALS AND PERHAPS SOME WILL BE CAREFULLY STORED AWAY AS NEXT SEASON'S SEED.

Frost is a rare commodity at Heligan but when it does come, *below,* in winter — rather than autumn or spring — hopefully for only short bursts, it is not to be begrudged as it takes plenty of bugs with it, and rarely does any significant harm.

ground it is a different story altogether. They are troubled by all manner of pests and diseases and have fussy nutritional requirements. Faced, as we are today, with supermarket shelves carrying an alluring range of such things as broccoli 'trees' and white cabbage, it is small wonder that the more accustomed varieties have their detractors. But in the Victorian era greens were a fact of life and you jolly well had to eat them up. All the problems of brassica crops, winter or summer, were also faced by the Victorians and much preventative or curative action, in particular the use of nets to protect crops, was the same then as it is today.

In the rotation scheme winter brassicas are planted in the patch from which potatoes have been removed. After the potato haulm is heaved away to the compost heap the ground is weeded, raked over and generally cleaned up. Once the lifting and sorting of potatoes has been carried out by Mike, Clive and Charles, most of the preparation

in readiness for the brassicas will be done by Haydn Smith and Annie Carr. Just before planting, the plot is graded to a proper level and walked over to provide firm soil conditions for the incoming plants. The larger brassicas such as the broccolis, kales and cauliflowers are top heavy for an inadequate root system and need to be planted in firm ground. They send down a single tap root off which grow tiny feeder roots but, because these roots are often not sufficient between them to support the plants through a wild and windy Cornish winter, sometimes the plants will have to be staked. But for the time being, all that is a long way off.

First, the seeds are sown in trays and given the best possible start in life in the heated propagation box which lives in the far corner of the Melon House. They germinate in under a week and are soon pricked out into modules (twelve cells in the size of a half seed tray) of peat-free compost, a necessary requirement as peat resources are effectively finite. Victorian composts used for seed raising in general (not for brassicas) differed greatly from ours. Unlike today, there was no tipping of ready-made compost from a bag onto the potting bench. More probably a mix was made up, by carefully combining grit and well-rotted leaf mould with material from a big supply of loam stacks. The business of procuring loam, or high-grade topsoil, from a stack of turf which had been piled grass side down was a big factor in Victorian methods of soil use. The turves were piled on top of one another to form a large bank, wide at the bottom and narrow at the top, to head height. They were then left to the elements so that the grass and the roots might rot down to produce loam.

For years the module-raised brassicas were planted directly into the soil, as I had been doing at Heligan during the early 1990s. The method now is to pot them up into nine-centimetre pots and grow them on to become much larger before planting out. Kathy Cartwright, whose brainchild this was, also opened everyone's eyes to the practice of potting the young plants deep in the nine-centimetre pot so that the larger leaves were low enough to be virtually touching the soil surface. This created a more vigorous root system, allowing the plant to get a better hold once it was in the ground. All this is as far removed as possible from the Victorian methods of raising

YOUNG BRASSICA PLANTS, *above,* PERKY AND UPRIGHT IN THEIR NINE-CENTIMETRE POTS ON THE LEDGE OF THE BACK WALL OF THE MELON HOUSE. FROM HERE THEY WILL BE TRANSFERRED TO A COLD FRAME TO HARDEN OFF, AND AFTER A COUPLE OF NIGHTS UNDER THE STARS THEY WILL BE PLANTED OUT.

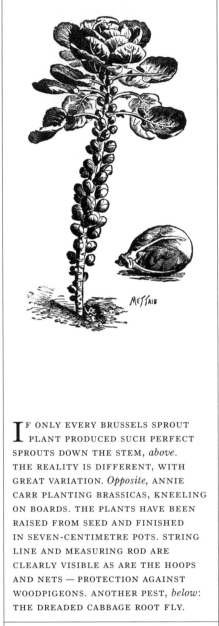

I F ONLY EVERY BRUSSELS SPROUT
PLANT PRODUCED SUCH PERFECT
SPROUTS DOWN THE STEM, *above.*
THE REALITY IS DIFFERENT, WITH
GREAT VARIATION. *Opposite,* ANNIE
CARR PLANTING BRASSICAS, KNEELING
ON BOARDS. THE PLANTS HAVE BEEN
RAISED FROM SEED AND FINISHED
IN SEVEN-CENTIMETRE POTS. STRING
LINE AND MEASURING ROD ARE
CLEARLY VISIBLE AS ARE THE HOOPS
AND NETS — PROTECTION AGAINST
WOODPIGEONS. ANOTHER PEST, *below*:
THE DREADED CABBAGE ROOT FLY.

winter brassicas. Then, all seed was sown in outside seedbeds, a practice still used at Heligan for cultivating wallflowers (which is also a
member of the brassica family), before the growing plants were lifted
and transplanted into their final position as required. This is a
perfectly acceptable way of raising brassica plants but growth is
slower, with more checking of development needed at transplanting.
The Victorians also sowed seed earlier, in March, at the same time as
the potatoes.

With just the right amount of nitrogen left by the preceding crop of
potatoes, when the brassica plants meet this fabulously fertile soil,
their rate of growth is prodigious. This, however, is when the trouble
starts. At planting, the base of each stem is 'collared' to stop the
cabbage root fly grubs eating the roots and killing the plant. Every
row of plants is then covered by a long net to keep out wood pigeons,
which have an insatiable appetite for brassicas. So, protected from the
bottom and the top the humble cabbage ventures further into the
world. By midsummer, when the plants have put on considerable
growth, the nets are removed; and this is when the next aerial threat
appears. Not only will the nets not keep them out, but the cabbage
white butterfly and the cabbage moth have similarly voracious
appetites to the wood pigeon. Over a day or two caterpillars can strip
an entire plant of its leaves. But the real problem arises when they eat
out the growing tip of the plant because regeneration does not happen
and the plant as a whole will not recover. To prevent severe damage
these pests have to be dealt with quickly and efficiently.

The whole process of growing brassicas to the standards set at
Heligan is extraordinarily time consuming and labour intensive.
It involves the gardeners spending a lot of time on boards and on their
knees and generally carrying out awkward tasks in difficult conditions
– but such are the joys of gardening that, however much they are put to
the test, their commitment is unfailing.

By the time autumn turns to winter, most of the brassica crops are
fully grown. Some now find their way to the Tea Room as an ingredient
in hot lunches for visitors to the gardens. A 'cabbage patch' is a slow-
burn undertaking, because some of the plants hold the ground for
almost a year. But when properly planned it can offer great value.
Meanwhile, by the time the last of the sprouting broccolis have given
up their juicy shoots in late spring of the following year, eleven months
after they were sown, it is time for the root crops, the second part of the
rotation, to take their place.

T HE WINTER CABBAGE PATCH
AT HELIGAN, *left*, REGULARLY
INVITES QUERIES AS TO HOW IT
LOOKS SO PERFECT. THE ANSWERS
ARE ALWAYS THE SAME: POT RAISE
THE PLANTS, DO NOT SOW THEM IN
SEED BEDS OUTSIDE, PROTECT THEM
WHEN YOUNG FROM PIGEONS AND
KEEP THE CATERPILLARS AT BAY WITH
THE BIOLOGICAL CONTROL BACTERIA
Bacillus thuringiensis. THE ADVENT OF
BIOLOGICAL CONTROLS HAS PROVED
A VERY VIABLE ALTERNATIVE TO
CHEMICAL CONTROLS OF CERTAIN
PESTS, SUCH AS CABBAGE WHITE
CATERPILLARS WHICH CAN RAVAGE
THE BRASSICA CROP. AS LARGE, WELL-
GROWN PLANTS THE PIGEONS FIND
THE BRASSICAS DIFFICULT TO COPE
WITH, EXCEPT IN EARLY SPRING,
WHEN THERE IS NOTHING ELSE TO
EAT AND THEY WILL RISK BALANCING
ON TOP OF THE PLANTS IN DAYLIGHT
HOURS WHEN THERE ARE PEOPLE
IN EVIDENCE.

Carrot Soup

Ingredients:
4 quarts of liquor in which
    a leg of mutton or beef
    has been boiled.
A few beef-bones.
6 large carrots.
2 large onions.
1 turnip.
Seasoning of salt and pepper
    to taste.
3 lumps of sugar.
Cayenne.

Mode. Put the liquor, bones, onions, turnip, pepper, and salt, into a stew-pan and simmer for 3 hours. Scrape and cut the carrots thin, strain the soup on them, and stew them till soft enough to pulp through a hair-sieve or coarse cloth; then boil the pulp with the soup, which should be of the consistency of pea-soup. Add cayenne. Pulp only the red part of the carrot, and make this soup the day before it is wanted.

CARROT SOUP FROM MY POINT OF VIEW IS MUCH IMPROVED BY THE ADDITION OF CUMIN (A HERB I HAVE TRIED AND FAILED TO GROW) RATHER THAN CORIANDER WHICH MANY SEEM TO PREFER. BUT FIRST YOU HAVE TO GROW YOUR CARROTS, WHICH IS THE HARDEST BIT OF ALL. I HAVE ALWAYS FOUND IT ODD THAT CARROTS WERE ALWAYS THE FIRST VEGETABLE SEED, BARRING RADISH, THAT WE WERE GIVEN TO GROW WHEN YOUNG, AS THEY CAN DISAPPOINT WITH STUNNING REGULARITY, FALLING FOUL OF THE SLIGHTEST HITCH IN TEMPERATURE AND SOIL CONDITIONS AND LAYING THEMSELVES BARE TO THE ATTENTIONS OF ALL MANNER OF PESTS AND DISEASES.

ROOT CROPS

It is easy to describe the soil in the Vegetable Garden at Heligan as fertile, and suitable for growing just about anything. The true test comes when the gardeners are faced with trying to grow root crops, in particular carrots. Many of the old-fashioned varieties of carrot that were grown in the Victorian era, some of them still in cultivation at Heligan today (such as Long Red Surrey), have long roots which travel deeply into the soil. (Modern varieties tend to be shallow rooting to enable harvesting by machine.) The purpose of rotating crops in the way that it is carried out at Heligan is not only to break any cycle of pests and disease and to build fertility but also to suit the nutritional requirements of each crop. To avoid problems with carrots and also to a certain extent parsnips, it is critical that the level of fertility is perfect.

This is how the rotation works: for potatoes the patch is trench dug, and well-rotted manure incorporated into the bottom of the trench. Potatoes are hungry, indeed they are known as gross feeders, and they will use up most of that added manure. The brassicas that follow are less hungry, so that there is still enough nitrogen left from the manure to feed their big green leaves. The root crops, on the other hand, have much less need for nitrogen; in fact an overload would cause the roots to 'fang', a term used to describe the splitting of the root as it searches for available nitrogen. If the rotation is followed correctly, so that the nutrient levels are right, the long roots of plants such as carrots, parsnips, salsify and scorzonera will grow straight and true. It is a fallacy that carrots will only grow in sandy soil – it is merely that there they will not encounter stones. But nor will they do so at Heligan, where the creation of the Vegetable Garden in the nineteenth century included the removal of any stones, probably as a job for the young boys employed in the gardens.

It is not certain when carrots were introduced as a culinary delicacy but there are references to them from the reign of Henry VIII, and in the glamorous court of King Charles, just over a century later, it was said that the ladies wore the foliage of the carrot as a substitute for feathers. Carrots were bred to

SYLVIA PULLS CARROTS FROM UNDER THE PROTECTIVE COVER OF HORTICULTURAL FLEECE, *below.* THE CURSE OF THE CARROT CROP, THE CARROT FLY, WILL DESTROY HEALTHY CROPS OF CARROTS IF NOT DEALT WITH. WHILST THE FLEECE IS ONLY PREVENTATIVE IT IS A VERY EFFECTIVE BARRIER IF SECURED PROPERLY — EVEN IF IT IS A LITTLE UNSIGHTLY.

take on an orange hue in Holland in the latter years of the same century under William of Orange, having come in a multitude of colours throughout history; the French, for example, being particularly fond of the purple carrot, *la carotte violette*.

The Victorian gardener was fastidious in his method of raising carrots. He felt certain that during the period of growth there should be virtually no cultivation, since any digging between the drills might lead to fanging. Only deep hoeing was allowed, in order to kill any weeds. A weed-infested row of carrots was unthinkable however. To combat this problem, carrot seed, which 'lies long in the ground', would be sown in a corner of the garden and allowed to germinate before being replanted in the required drill. In this way it stole a march on any weeds that might otherwise germinate faster than the carrots themselves. Such attention to detail took an astonishing amount of labour and time, much as the same remarkable pursuit of the highest possible standards is in practice at Heligan today.

The sowing of the first root crops begins as early as February in the Vegetable Garden, whose produce includes maincrop varieties. The moment the ground is dry enough to work, the soil is lightly forked over rather than dug, then weeded and graded to a fine tilth suitable for direct seed sowing. Grading is a fine art, but Heligan's gardeners have become practised in finding a level as they grade. They use a wide rake with rounded aluminium teeth which can move large amounts of topsoil at a time while creating a fine tilth. This sounds easy, but it is not. To get a proper level over the entire plot you have to look at that plot as a whole while trying to smooth out any peaks and troughs as you go. Grading before potato planting, for example, can be a nightmare as the plot is one mass of ridges where the soil has been trench dug so that every level is wrong. First a smaller rake is used to break down any large clods and push the soil around to some sort of level, working from the top to the bottom of the entire bed. Then comes the landscape rake to put the finishing touches to the job.

As soon as this is completed, a line of string is set up along the full length of the row to be sown. Walking boards are placed a few inches away from the line – again the full length of the row. The boards are odd lengths of skirting and other assorted bits of timber salvaged from around the estate. All seed sowing is carried out from boards to prevent compacting the soil. Over the years Kathy Cartwright and now Sylvia Travers have begun to use a tape measure when sowing seed and planting out. Most of the beds are around 30 metres across and for extreme

THE FIBROUS AND WOODY CORE OF THE PARSNIP, *above,* IS EDIBLE BUT COARSE AND LACKING IN FLAVOUR, UNLIKE THE SWEET SURROUNDING FLESH. OVERSIZE ROOTS WERE FED TO HORSES FOR THE HIGH SUGAR CONTENT. VERY HARDY, PARSNIPS CAN STAY IN THE SOIL OVER WINTER WITHOUT INCURRING DAMAGE.

YLVIA BEARS AN ARMFUL OF
PERFECT SIZED PARSNIPS *below*.
SWEET AND AROMATIC, THEY ARE
ONE OF THE FIRST CROPS TO BE SOWN
IN SPRING, AS JEREMY PEDERSEN
DEMONSTRATES *bottom right*, KNEEL-
ING ON THE BOARDS WITH THE YOUNG
ROWS OF THE PEA 'VEITCH'S WESTERN
EXPRESS' IN THE BACKGROUND.

accuracy of sowing the tape is run the full length of the row, tight to the string line. This is particularly useful for parsnips as the papery seeds are difficult to sprinkle and are better placed, two and a half centimetres apart, in the rows. Such precision and attention to detail has become a trademark of the Heligan productive gardens over the years and whilst it is time consuming it does yield the best possible results.

Parsnips are cussed germinators. They like the soil to be warm, at least ten degrees centigrade; but the purpose of sowing early is to achieve the really long roots that as full as possible a season will allow. In the nineteenth century parsnips were fed to horses for their high sugar content, and the bigger they could be grown the better. However, germination is not always guaranteed and a spell of cold wet weather

can further restrict it, so that sometimes a second sowing may be required. In our time this is not seen as too disastrous because with no horses to feed there is less of a requirement for giant roots. These, in turn, can be a problem in autumn, when they are very difficult to dig from the ground without the root ends breaking off.

Whatever the uncertainties of waiting for the parsnips to germinate, once they are up and away they present few problems; indeed there could not be an easier crop to grow. As soon as the seedlings are showing, and are large enough to handle, a first thinning of the row takes place. Mike Rundle dons knee pads and sets off up the row on hands and knees, thinning the seedlings to about seven to ten centimetres apart. This done, the rows are watered back in to settle everything down. A second and final thinning takes place once the plants are 15–20 centimetres high. It is then that the bruised leaves give off that sweet smoky smell so peculiar to the parsnip. Many other members of the apiaceae family also have strongly scented leaves, be they carrots, celery or wild hedgerow herbs such as alexanders.

The cultivation of carrots, the other mainstay of the root section, is largely similar except that these suffer badly from the attentions of a virulent pest in the form of carrot fly. This infuriating insect is attracted by the smell of the carrot and on locating the source will lay eggs at the base of the plant. When the grubs hatch, they burrow into the soil and from there into the carrot itself. A bad infestation of carrot fly will result in near-total crop failure, and measures to combat this danger are limited without the use of chemicals. The problem centres around the fact that the hedgerows and the garden in general are full of members of the same family of plants, which act as hosts to the fly. Rotation helps to improve the situation, but year on year the fly will return and find the carrots come what may, so that various means of control have to be devised. Over the years the entire crop has been covered with horticultural fleece as a preventative barrier; but it only takes one gale in the night to lift a portion of the fleece, whereupon the fly can and will get in. Also, having large swathes of the Vegetable Garden covered in a white blanket during the summer does not present an attractive sight. However, if the fleece can be prevented from blowing away or tearing, it does form a very effective preventative barrier.

The latest breakthrough in the battle against carrot fly is a biological control. This takes the form of a nematode which lays its eggs inside the carrot fly's grub. It is similar in essence to the nematode which is used to combat slugs. A bacterium to kill the caterpillars of the

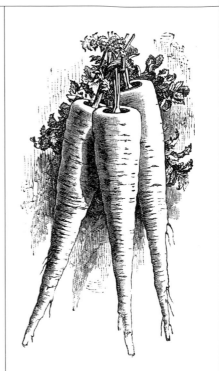

THEY SCRUB UP WELL. FRESHLY WASHED AND SCRUBBED PARSNIPS SNUGGLE UP NEXT TO HEADS OF CELERIAC, *left*, AND AWAIT THEIR JOURNEY UP TO THE TEA ROOM FOR CONSUMPTION AS LUNCH. IT IS SOMETHING OF A MATTER OF PRIDE FOR THE GARDENERS THAT ALL BAR THE VERY UNUSUAL AND UNPALATABLE OF THE FRUITS AND VEGETABLES GROWN AT HELIGAN FIND THEIR WAY TO THE KITCHENS OF THE TEA ROOM. WHILST MOST OF THE PRODUCE IS LEFT AS LONG AS POSSIBLE IN THE GARDEN TO GARNER MAXIMUM VISUAL EFFECT, IT ALL GETS THERE IN THE END. *Below*, THE CARROT FLY.

Always remember to wash
your hands after handling
horseradish, *above,* and certainly
before rubbing your eyes. it
is hot and it burns. beetroot,
opposite, is framed by the giant
ornamental trees that surround
the vegetable garden. the
double stemmed conifer is a
westerbn red cedar (Thuja plicata).
to its right is the douglas fir
with its witches' broom. *Below,*
the cabbage white butterfly in
its three stages of growth. the
caterpillar is the one to watch
— it is a fast-growing and
extremely hungry creature and
one of the most destructive of
all horticultural pests.

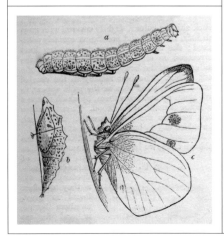

cabbage white butterfly is also in use and has proved very successful over the years. Any method of pest and disease control which reduces the need for chemicals is to be applauded. The Victorians may well have used a chemical had they been able to procure one but for them it was most often a case of trying to comprehend the life cycle and habits of the pest in question. With the dreaded carrot fly it was important to time the sowing of the carrot crop to avoid the peak emergence of the first generation of adult flies; this is normally around the end of May when the cow parsley is in full flower. As it is the scent of the carrot plant that attracts the adult egg-carrying females, gardeners were no doubt careful when it came to thinning the crop. This was probably carried out towards evening when the fly was less active in the air, with the thinnings being swiftly removed from the rows.

Because of the ample size of the Tea Room at Heligan, where everything sent from the Vegetable Garden gets eaten up quickly, there is not much need for crops to be stored over winter. The gardeners who supplied the kitchens of Heligan House, however, would have made storage an important part of vegetable and fruit growing, and root crops would have been set by in bulk. Carrots were best stored in a cellar in dry sand having been lifted on a day when the excess soil was itself dry enough to be knocked off the roots. The tops were cut off and even a small slice of the crown removed, to stop the plant regrowing. Some gardeners would singe the sliced crown with a hot iron to seal the wound and prevent regrowth. Perhaps a shovel full of hot coals would be brought up from the Vinery boiler room to carry out this practice. There was talk in those days of carrots lasting up to two years in clamps underground, the same method that was used for potatoes. Parsnips, being much less prone to frost damage than carrots, are left in the ground and lifted as and when required. Beetroots, when lifted, are used at once, although the Victorians also stored them in sand, making sure, since they 'bleed', to cut the tops off a few centimetres above the crown.

While carrots and parsnips make up most of the rotation system for roots, there are less usual crops which also belong here. Salsify and scorzonera are two old-fashioned kinds of root which are becoming more popular. Both have a distinctive smoky flavour and are grown in much the same way as parsnips. The variety of salsify, a member of the daisy family, which is grown at Heligan is Sandwich Island, dating from 1898. The mature root, although not as long, is similar in shape to the parsnip; it differs in that it produces a number of extra roots which grow off the taproot. There are also numerous root hairs, but these are

THE ROOT ROTATION, *above*. A CRITICAL ROTATION IN VICTORIAN VEGETABLE GARDENS AS MUCH FOR THE STORAGE POTENTIAL OF THE ROOTS AS FOR THE ROTATION ITSELF. THE ACTION OF THE ROOTS' GROWTH, ESPECIALLY PARSNIPS, BREAKS UP THE SOIL AND DRAWS UP NUTRIENTS AND MINERALS FROM THE SUBSOIL WHICH WILL ULTIMATELY BE RETURNED TO THE TOPSOIL VIA THE COMPOSTED WASTE MATTER OF THE PLANTS.

easily trimmed off. The best way to cook salsify is to parboil or gently steam the root and then roast it in good olive oil until crisp on the outside and soft in the middle, again like a parsnip. Scorzonera is a native of Spain and cultivated in much the same way as salsify. The variety grown at Heligan is Maxima. This has a straight black root about the thickness of a wooden spoon handle and is best cooked like salsify: parboiled and then roasted. With both vegetables, as is the general rule of thumb when cultivating root crops, it is essential to thin the seedlings to the required spacings which should be 15 centimetres apart if the roots are to maximize their potential.

More demanding for the gardeners is the cultivation of chicory. To most people the production of Belgian or Witloof chicory is a mystery. A huge percentage of us buy the white and yellow pointed chicons 'ready made' from supermarkets, with no clue how they are produced.

Dressed Salsify

Ingredients:

Salsify.

To each ½ gallon of water allow 1 heaped tablespoonful of salt, 1 oz. of butter, 2 tablespoonfuls of lemon juice.

Mode: Scrape the roots gently, so as to strip them only of their outside peel; cut them into pieces about 4 inches long, and, as they are peeled, throw them into water with which has been mixed a little lemon-juice, to prevent their discolouring. Put them into boiling water, with salt, butter and lemon-juice in the above proportion, and let them boil rapidly until tender; try them with a fork; and, when it penetrates easily, they are done. Drain the salsify, and serve with a good white sauce or French melted butter.

IT PLEASES ME NO END THAT SALSIFY IS MAKING A COMEBACK BEYOND THE REALMS OF THE VICTORIAN KITCHEN GARDEN AND I DARE SAY HELIGAN HAS HAD QUITE A BIT TO DO WITH THAT. IT IS A DELICACY IF COOKED PROPERLY AND CAN MAKE PARSNIPS LOOK VERY WORKMANLIKE AND UNCOUTH. IT IS EASY TO GROW BUT DOES COME OUT OF THE GROUND BOTH HAIRY AND MISSHAPEN; DO NOT LET THAT PUT YOU OFF.

Perpetual spinach and swiss chard, *above,* provide much needed green matter beyond brassica crops. Unable to fit into the rotation per se, a home is found for them amongst the miscellaneous crops which make up their own rotation of the same name. They are also used as a catch crop after the early legumes and are ceaselessly popular with the staff and the kitchens.

To Sylvia, Annie and Haydn in the Vegetable Garden the production of a beautifully formed head of chicory is a job well done, for this is no easy task. The first stage involves sowing seed a few centimetres apart in the late spring. The small lettuce-like plants which emerge are thinned once, and then again to a final spacing of about 30 centimetres. Thereafter they are allowed to grow freely throughout the summer, producing abundant conical green foliage like that of a giant cos lettuce. A trouble-free crop, the chicory plants continue growing until the autumn, when their growth slows and they have produced an enormous parsnip-like root underneath the top-heavy foliage. At this point the plant is dug up.

This is where the clever bit comes in. The foliage is cut off, two centimetres above the top of the roots, of which only the straight and vigorous are selected for forcing. The roots are cleaned off, placed upright in 30-centimetre-wide terracotta pots and packed with sand to hold them steady. Another 30-centimetre pot is placed over the top of the one which holds the roots, and the pots are then placed under the staging in the Potting Shed, where the temperature is roughly 55 degrees Fahrenheit. Within two weeks the first chicons will start to appear from the top or crown of the roots; but if the temperature drops much lower the roots will not produce any new growth. Because of the mild Cornish climate the roots are often left until the late autumn; they are then lifted, and chucked in the corner of the lean-to before anything is done with them. This can mean that the chicons will not be produced until the spring, when the temperature warms up.

This puts me in mind of how the first chicons of forced chicory are said to have come about. Allegedly, a Belgian farmer was growing chicory as cattle fodder. Having let his cows graze off the chicory tops in the field he lifted the roots to store them as winter feed. During the course of the winter months, as the huge stockpile of chicory began to diminish, he began to notice signs of growth on the top of the roots. As he delved into the pile, where the temperature was higher and the darkness had been deeper, he found a number of huge white chicons, and a new winter salad crop was born.

Blanching was an important aspect of Victorian vegetable gardening. Asparagus was mounded up to whiten and sweeten the lower part of the stems, and celery was even wrapped with brown paper to make the stems pale and crunchy. This is still done at Heligan today and is one of many unusual horticultural practices which invite comment from the visiting public. Today, self-blanching varieties of celery are available, but these compare unfavourably with the product which has been wrapped by hand. What an extraordinary process this is. Like many members of the apiaceae family, celery, and its relation celeriac, are obtuse in their habits. They are poor germinators, much like carrots and parsnips, and they feel the cold. Celery is raised from seed in the Melon House and grown on until it is time to plant it out, when the weather must be warm. If it is too cold the plants, both celery and celeriac, will sit and refuse to grow until the weather and the soil do warm up, when they promptly bolt. It can be frustrating to consider the great lengths that have been gone to in making sure that everything is in place for them. Celeriac, the rooting form of celery, is merely planted out in rows and allowed to grow on through the summer; but for celery there is more to do.

To begin with, Clive digs a trench the width of his shovel and 30 centimetres deep, and banks the soil up on either side. The young plants are placed in the bottom of the trench and grown on until they are about 30 centimetres tall, when they are wrapped in brown paper and tied up with raffia. At this point the trench is filled in around the celery parcels, so that all that can be seen poking through the surface

Not dissimilar to the root of a parsnip, witloof chicory, *above*, is the finest of all the winter salads. It grows in the root rotation as much for its mode of growing as for anything else, but it is a delicacy like asparagus, *below*, which is considerably easier to grow.

are the tufts of the top of the plants and a little brown paper. They remain this way until the autumn, when they are uncovered and harvested, by which time they are blanched, sweet and very fat.

Any confusion between the terms blanching and forcing must be swiftly cleared up. Both were common practice in Victorian horticulture and, as we have just seen, blanching is still very much in use. Forcing is something quite different and describes the production of a crop out of season and often in extreme circumstances such as with added heat.

The Melon Yard holds a forcing room, which is found underneath the Fruit Room; the two levels are collectively known as the 'two-storied building'. Currently the forcing room is used to grow mushrooms; but it is highly likely that in the Victorian era it was used for forcing a variety of crops. These are likely to have included such delicacies as asparagus and rhubarb, and even the delicately scented and much-admired lily-of-the valley. The crucial elements for indoor forcing were heat and darkness. Both were required for crops like asparagus and sea kale, the darkness providing the blanching and the heat enabling the crop to be brought on before its natural outdoor growing season. Hotbeds were also used as a means of forcing. By a simple process a quantity of horse manure, maybe a trailer load, was turned continually until a peak of fermentation was reached. This was tested by inserting a hand into the heap – a hazardous operation. The manure was then placed in an empty cold frame or on the soil in the garden,

IT IS THE BEST OF ALL POSSIBLE WORLDS FOR THESE BUNCHES OF CELERIAC DEPICTED BY THE VICTORIAN ILLUSTRATOR, *above*. IF ONLY SMOOTH ROOTS WERE THE NORM. THE REALITY IS A MASSED TANGLE OF ROOT AND SOIL, MAKING PREPARATION A NIGHTMARE. *Right*, THE LINE OF SEA KALE FORCING POTS.

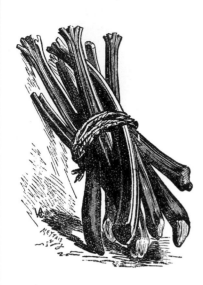

Rhubarb, *above,* has many fans but also many detractors. However, they would surely be won over if they could see the fluorescent pink of the stems that emerge from under the forcers, *above right,* and taste the sweetness. The straw serves a multitude of purposes. It holds moisture around plants which have a considerable requirement for water; it controls weeds and prevents soil erosion; it bulks up around the crowns and protects the plants from frost before being scraped away to make room for the forcer.

and a layer of soil deep enough for sowing seeds was placed on top. The heat produced rapid growth and, if blanching was not required, hotbeds could also be used for asparagus and rhubarb.

A common association made today with the Victorian garden is that of the large terracotta 'forcing' pot. These bell-shaped jars, designed for blanching sea kale and allied with the taller conical-shaped pots used for rhubarb, are excellent for blanching and thereby sweetening crops. Using a large heap of fermenting manure, it would be possible to pile this around the pots covering dormant crowns of rhubarb and sea kale, and force the crop into an earlier growth.

The root stage of rotation can also include one or two brassicas. Strictly speaking they should not be there, but the cultivation of turnips and winter radish is as root crops and there is no other obvious place for them. After potatoes, brassicas and roots the soil needs a boost and this is provided in the third year by the legume section of the rotation, namely peas and beans.

PEAS AND BEANS

It cannot be coincidence that the four main plant groups making up the bulk of our dietary needs also happen to make up the four principal sections of the rotation. The fact that at Heligan there are six courses in the rotation is by choice. The pumpkins and squashes are a relatively new addition and alliums – the onion family – were always maintained

Boiled Sea Kale

Ingredients:
Sea kale.
To each ½ gallon of water allow 1 heaped teaspoonful of salt.

Mode. Well wash the kale, cut away any worm eaten pieces, and tie it into small bunches; put it into boiling water, salted in the above proportion, and let it boil quickly until tender. Take it out, drain, untie the bunches, and serve with plain melted butter or white sauce, a little of which may be poured over the kale. Sea-kale may also be par-boiled and stewed in good brown gravy: it will then take about ½ hour altogether.

SEA KALE, ALONG WITH ASPARA-GUS, IS THE BEST VEGETABLE IN THE GARDEN. PURPLE SPROUTING BROCCOLI AND THE SPROUTING KALE 'PENTLAND BRIG' TIE FOR THIRD PLACE. THE IMPORTANT THING IS TO GROW IT YOURSELF: THE BOUGHT PRODUCT DOES NOT MEASURE UP BECAUSE THE FLAVOUR TURNS UNPLEASANT HOURS AFTER THE STEMS ARE CUT. IT IS VERY PUNGENT WITH AN ALMOST ACRID SMELL TO IT IN THE KIND OF EGGY WAY THAT BRASSICAS HAVE ABOUT THEM. CUT AND COOKED QUICKLY AND SLATHERED IN BUTTER — OR BETTER STILL, HOLLANDAISE SAUCE — IT IS A CRUNCHY, SAVOURY JOY.

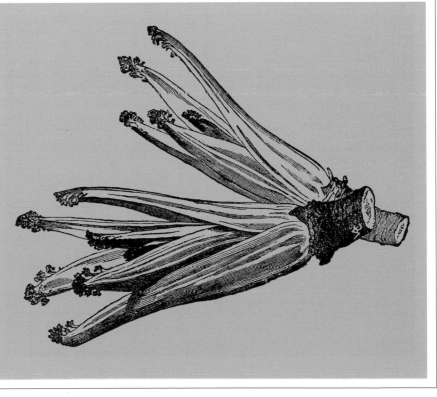

in a 'Miscellaneous' fifth course which took care of other odd bits and pieces such as overflow flower bulbs and salads.

Of the four large crops, potatoes provide carbohydrates; greens, fibre; carrots and roots, essential vitamins; while legumes supply protein. A vegetarian diet, as we know, is more than adequate for perfect health. It is noteworthy, then, that the foundations of human health are also the basis of soil health.

The importance of legumes for the soil, upon which both crop and human health are entirely dependent, is that they replace the nitrogen of which it has been robbed by the three preceding crops. It is always a marvel to me that, in some plant species, atmospheric nitrogen can be taken up, and held in bacteria which live in small nodules on their roots. Yet this is what legumes do. They are then able to release the stored nitrogen in their roots for their own nourishment – and for that of other plants, in our case the following crop of alliums.

The Victorians had a firm grasp of the importance of legumes and were keen on the broad bean as not only a delicacy but as a garden-worthy plant with a number of incidentally useful attributes. The beans stored well, the plants, being able to produce their own nourishment, were strong growers in most soils and there were ample varieties and a wide range of colours to suit most growers. This is still true, and the longpods and Windsors are as popular today as they have ever been.

In many respects the legume crop marks the beginning of the growing year at Heligan in the Vegetable Garden, because the first of the spring broad beans to become ready will actually have been sown during the previous autumn. It takes considerable skill on the part of Sylvia and her staff to nurse them through the winter. One reason why they are vulnerable is that during the lean months they are one of the few plants in the garden providing fresh young growth as food for hungry birds and mammals. Mice can be a problem; so 'humane' traps are set and any captives released in the garden's Woodland Walk. Rooks, which live in the big cryptomeria between the Flower Garden and Heligan House, have also been known to show interest in small tender bean growth. Curiously, rather than eat the tips of the plants they simply nip them off and leave them on the surface of the soil, as an act of wilful hooliganism.

As a result of this even the broad beans, the sturdiest and hardiest of growers, have to be netted in their early days as protection against the ever-growing ranks of increasingly determined garden pests. In the early part of summer 2005, after a prolonged spell of dry weather

SEED SAVING IS AN ESSENTIAL PART OF THE ETHOS OF THE PRODUCTIVE GARDENS, *right*. POTATOES AND PEAS AND BEANS ARE PERHAPS THE MOST OBVIOUS ONES TODAY, BUT THE WHOLE BUSINESS WAS SOMETHING PRACTISED BY THE VICTORIANS AS MUCH AS POSSIBLE. SEED WAS (AND STILL IS) EXPENSIVE AND HAD TO TRAVEL LONG DISTANCES TO CORNWALL SO ALL MANNER OF SEEDS WERE SAVED. THE PICTURE SHOWS FRENCH BEANS AND ALSO ONIONS AT THE BOTTOM. LABORIOUS BUT WORTHWHILE, AS SOME PERIOD-CORRECT SEEDS ARE VERY HARD TO COME BY.

Sowing and planting the
legumes, *above* and *right*. Broad
beans and peas are easy to grow
from seed as are runner beans.
French beans are notoriously
difficult from a direct sowing
and they are grown in pots and
planted out. the proximity to the
cut flower beds leads to massive
problems with slugs in summer,
the warm and often wet
conditions proving troublesome.
the problem is increasingly
effectively dealt with by
a biological control.

through late May and early June, a whole row of mature broad beans
was completely destroyed by blackbirds who, it was thought, came
after the beans in search of moisture. No one had ever seen the like of it
and when Haydn came in first thing in the morning he found that
the whole row was shaking under a frantic attack from the birds.
He described it as a feeding frenzy, with the empty shells of the beans
scattered everywhere.

But the good news is that there is nothing compromising about such
ravages. Most of the damage done to the crops in the Vegetable Garden
is 'mechanical', by which I mean that it is done by something large
such as a wood pigeon or a rabbit rather than by a disease, introduced
through unsound horticultural practices. By contrast though, some of
those creatures that do trouble the crops are becoming slier and more
cunning by the year. I have seen rabbits scale the metre-high fence
designed to keep them out, having failed to clear it by jumping.
Similarly pigeons can land among the brassicas in broad daylight, with
people everywhere, and bide their time before beginning to peck at the
plants, in the knowledge that their landing was unnoticed.

The autumn-sown broad beans, Aquadulce Claudia, spend their
winter under the protective net. There they put up with the wind and
weather and never reach more than about 20 centimetres in height,
having stopped growing through the month of January. Although a
trouble-free crop in general, during the course of their growing season
the broad beans can throw out three minor distress signals.

As mature plants the beans, without fail, will be visited by a small
weevil, a species of flying beetle, which will dine off the edges of the
foliage, leaving tiny semi-circular bite marks and a missing bit of leaf.
Some weevils are perfect menaces throughout the horticultural industry.
The vine weevil in particular can cause havoc amongst containerised
plants such as primulas. In contrast the pea and bean weevil is relatively
harmless: its contribution of mechanical damage to the plants looks
almost comically regular but at least it does no significant harm.

Next up is a fungal disease called chocolate spot, which is caused by
a deficiency of potash in the soil. Potash – or to give its scientific name,
potassium, signified by the letter 'k' in the table of elements – is one of
the three main elements essential to plant growth, the other two being
nitrogen and phosphorous. It is readily available through wood ashes,
compost, stable manure and seaweed, but it is also highly water soluble
and as such is 'leached' through the soil, in other words drained off,
over the winter by the large quantity of rain that falls in Cornwall.

This is one of the reasons that we try to cover as much soil as possible in the Vegetable Garden with seaweed during the course of the winter, as this produces a mulch that helps prevent leaching. One of the few problems associated with the rotation system practised in the Heligan Vegetable Garden is that over the winter by necessity there are large areas of soil left bare and uncovered. Much of the ground has to be trench dug, a process that takes a great deal of time, and therefore it is not practical to cover the soil with seaweed until this job is complete. However, I should point out that where the soil at Heligan might be

THE FIRST OF THE SUMMER'S PRO-
DUCE, THE AUTUMN SOWN BROAD
BEAN AQUADULCE CLAUDIA, *left,* IS
SURELY ONE OF THE MOST DELICIOUS.
TENDER AND JUICY, IT IS THE CLASSIC
EXAMPLE OF A VEGETABLE BEING AT
ITS BEST WHEN SMALL AND IMMATURE.
THE RED-FLOWERED BROAD BEAN,
right, IS A COLOURFUL ADDITION TO
THE RANKS. CROSS-POLLINATION
WITHIN THE ROW IS AVOIDED BY
ROGUEING OUT ANY WHITE FLOWERED
PLANTS THAT MAY HAVE ARRIVED BY
ACCIDENT. *Below,* SEVILLE LONGPOD
BEANS.

found to suffer a potash deficiency the fact is that the broad bean is very greedy for this mineral. In gardening, mineral deficiencies cannot always be anticipated by rule of thumb.

Chocolate spot marks the leaves with striking brown areas of rich discolouration, but tends not to appear until the plants have reached full maturity and the bean crop has mostly been harvested. Although it weakens the plants it is not by any means disastrous. However, this damage to the cell structure prepares the way for attack by black aphid. Although a common pest of broad beans in general, this insect is particularly attracted by a weakening plant which, by the very fact that it is a legume and growing in nitrogen-rich soil, is still full of this mineral. Thankfully the growing cycle is virtually complete by this time and the tips of the plants, where the attack takes place, will have been pinched out by the gardeners in the course of harvesting.

Successional sowing means, in the case of broad beans, the cultivation of different varieities to ensure a constant supply through the summer. It ensures different sizes of plant, different colours of seed and flower and the confident knowledge that work is being done to replenish the precious stocks of nitrogen needed each year if the garden is to show its full potential. There are longpod varieties, Windsors, red-flowered beans, and even a dwarf variety, called 'the Sutton'. The last named is best known for its use as a 'catch crop': one that, as well as lifting nitrogen levels while producing a harvest of its own, can be used to fill a piece of blank ground in between the cycle of other crops.

Runner beans are a stalwart of every English vegetable garden. They are unusual because they are the only annual vegetable crop which is considered safe to grow in the same piece of ground year after year. This curious-sounding traditional practice is one that is still followed today. The four long rows at Heligan run the full length of the Vegetable Garden, on either side of the north-south path that lies just beyond the cut-flower beds. It has always been held amongst the staff here that once Mike Rundle starts putting up the bean canes, spring has arrived.

The other half of the rotation's legume section is taken up by peas. These, to my mind, have created a certain sense of the unique in the Heligan Vegetable Garden. Row upon row of two-metre-tall nineteenth-century varieties of pea plant leave one in no doubt that this is the real article. Its uniqueness has indeed set the standards for anyone else trying to replicate a Victorian vegetable garden.

REGIMENTATION AND ABUNDANCE. THE HIGH SUMMER ABUNDANCE IN THE PEA AND BEAN ROWS, BRACED BY POLES, WIRE AND STRING, *below left,* IS TEMPERED BY AN EARLIER STARK SHOT ACROSS THE YOUNG ANTIRRHINUMS, *right.* THE ATTENTION TO DETAIL AND PRECISE MEASUREMENT IS REPRESENTATIVE OF HELIGAN'S GARDENING ETHOS; AND THE PERSISTENCE IN GROWING VICTORIAN VARIETIES, OFTEN LABOUR-INTENSIVE, IS ANOTHER OF THE GARDEN'S HALLMARKS. *Below,* A PODDED FRENCH RUNNER BEAN.

Peas, *below*, WERE SUCH AN IMPOR-
TANT CROP FOR THE VICTORIANS,
AS SHOWN BY THE ENORMOUS NUMBER
OF VARIETIES AVAILABLE. NOT ONLY
DID THEY PROVIDE IMPORTANT
PROTEIN, THEY ALSO REPLACED THE
PRECIOUS NITROGEN ROBBED BY THE
PRECEDING CROPS IN THE GARDEN.

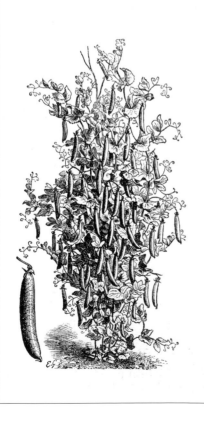

Of all the crops grown at Heligan peas are, however, the most recal-
citrant. Soon after sowing, in early spring, they push through the
ground with great purpose, only to be eaten by pigeons. It rains and the
slugs come. The supports are inadequate and the stems bend and snap.
The plants are martyrs to mildew, and then what's left of the crop gives
itself up to the pea moth. There is always some setback to do with the
peas. Yet, since the high hedges they make were a reliable feature of
Victorian gardening, that is how they are cultivated at Heligan, invit-
ing by their very growth perhaps more comment than any other crop.
The long rows of Ne Plus Ultra, Magnum Bonum, Champion of
England and Veitch's Western Express make an impressive sight as
they tower over the neighbouring broad beans. But they do require a
lot of work, beginning with netting against the aerial threat of pigeons.
Mice must be trapped; and throughout all levels of their growing cycle
the plants must be staked, culminating in the need for full-length
hazel-twig supports tied to a system of posts and wires that runs all the
way up the 33-metre beds. The pea crop presents the gardeners with a
continuing series of trials, but when at cropping time great trugs of
peas are filled and distributed it is with a great sense of a job well done.

The earliest crop of peas is started in January and sown in boxes:
Veitch's Western Express will be planted out as seedlings and does not
have to risk being eaten by any mice that may come looking for directly
sown seed. Here the Heligan method is right on the trail of the Victorians.
A famous gardener and author of the eighteenth century named Justice
recorded in the British Gardener's Calendar in 1759 that peas cropped
much better when transplanted from boxes, as this shortened the long
tap root, allowing for a much stronger rooting system to develop.
In all likelihood this was a practice continued into the Victorian era.

After harvesting both the peas and the broad beans, the haulm, as
the foliage is known, is cut off near enough at ground level and any
remaining nitrogen allowed to find its way into the soil. Then, as
autumn moves in, as soon as enough people are free, a series of runs
will begin down to Portmellon beach, with the hope that during the
winter the entire plot can be covered in seaweed as a mulch to protect
its precious nitrogen.

And yet for all this attention to tradition, the few varieties of pea
grown at Heligan are almost nothing compared to what was to be had
in the Victorian era. At one point, in about 1862, the Horticultural
Society entrusted a Mr Gordon to cultivate and trial all available
varieties in order to clear up any confusion on the nomenclature of

The earliest of the season's peas, 'veitch's western express', is covered against the woodpigeon threat by young beech twigs, *below. Bottom right,* they have reached well over two metres in height and are supported by much bigger hazel twigs and in turn by wire and string. clive mildenhall, *top right,* puts up a teepee which will also have peas growing up the canes.

the garden pea. Mr Gordon divided peas into nine groups including dwarfs, marrows (related to the marrowfats we know today), talls, Russians, Imperials, sugars and grey common. Within these groups most of the varieties were very likely tasteless; but it was characteristic of developments in horticulture at that time that, in due course, standards got considerably better.

The practicalities of large-scale vegetable gardening can be summed up in two words: labour intensive. The constant round of hoeing, staking and general maintenance, such as early-morning raking along the paths, is mere punctuation in the drive towards optimum soil fertility and maximum crop yields. There are few chances to break from the routine without risking a breakdown in the system. The cyclical nature of the growing season means that most tasks must be carried out

punctually, a constraint that calls for focus and determination. It also calls for an understanding of just why each task has to be done in the present and not the near future. Year on year it becomes ever clearer to visitors that this attention to detail combined with plain hard graft is the key to success. This too is what makes the Heligan productive gardens so extraordinary, in a way that is a huge reward for the gardeners whose steady work has brought them to such a pitch of excellence.

THE ONION FAMILY

The onion crop is only one of several members from the allium family that are grown in profusion at Heligan. From a handful of varieties it has progressed to being, in a historical perspective, one of the most important crops grown here. In the early 1990s the only period-correct onion in the garden was Stuttgart Giant, which dated from the 1890s. It was grown from sets, small immature onions, established during the previous year and then bought in. The production of onions from sets is straightforward – the little bulblets are pushed into the ground as soon as soil conditions are suitable, in late February or March. The crop grows on, and the mature bulbs are lifted in early August to be stored away for the winter.

By the late 1990s Philip had decided that we could do better. He turned for help to Heritage Seedsman Thomas Etty Esq're, the opening words of whose catalogue are 'Mr Etty begs (most respectfully) to bring to the notice of the Nobility, Gentry, Clergy and Others, this is his annual specialist seed catalogue. In doing so he trusts that his determination to select from none but the best stocks will ensure for him the patronage which it will be his anxious study to merit.'

There, for perusal on page 6, can be found an extensive collection of heritage onion varieties, all available by seed rather than sets and with dates of introduction. Allen's Reliance, which dates from 1880, the catalogue informs us, 'was selected by Mr Allen, gardener to Lord Suffield from seed of onions bought at the Nottingham Goose Fair and brought up to the very highest type of white Spanish'. Ailsa Craig, introduced in 1887, is listed as being 'a large and handsome variety. The skin is a pale straw colour. The flesh is white. The bulbs are irregular in form, some being globe shaped, others inclined to a flat oval. Seed should be started in a hot bed or in a box in a house for their full development'. Otherwise seed was sown outside in a seedbed in early spring and transplanted on reaching a suitable size.

ONIONS HAVE PICKED UP IN POPULARITY AT HELIGAN, AND THE NUMBER OF VARIETIES HAS ALSO INCREASED. THE OLD-FASHIONED ONIONS THAT ARE PERIOD-CORRECT FOR HELIGAN'S COMMITTED STYLE OF NINETEENTH-CENTURY HORTICULTURE ARE LARGELY AVAILABLE FOR CULTIVATION ONLY FROM SEED AND THIS MAKES THE TASK LABORIOUS AND DELICATE. ONCE THEY REACH THE SOIL THEY ARE USUALLY UNTROUBLED, EXCEPT BY MILDEW, WHICH CAN INTERRUPT GROWTH CONSIDERABLY, AT MATURITY, WHEN THE FOLIAGE BEGINS TO LOOK AGED AND THE SKIN OF THE ONION IS MAKING ITS PAPER COAT, *left,* THEY ARE PULLED AND LAID ON THE SURFACE.

JAMES LONG KEEPING, *left,* IS GROWN
HERE FOR SEED PRODUCTION. IT
WILL BE GROWN THROUGH THE
SEASON, ALLOWED TO FLOWER AND
SET SEED AND THEN BE PULLED,
DRIED OFF AND THE SEED REMOVED
FOR SAFE KEEPING. SEED SAVING IS
INCREASINGLY BECOMING PART OF
HORTICULTURE AT HELIGAN; IT CER-
TAINLY WAS UNDER THE VICTORIANS.

Not a great deal has changed since 1880; in fact this procedure is precisely what happens today. Sylvia sows the seed in modules rather than trays, which she then places on the surface of the empty melon and cucumber beds in the Melon House. Hidden underneath the big slabs of Delabole slate which make up the flooring of the bed is a soil-warming cable system which runs off electricity. Cheating yes, but it mimics the action of the hotbed by simply replacing fermenting manure with electricity. Two or three seeds are sown at a time and the two weakest pricked out to leave a single onion plant in its little cell. It stays there until planting time, usually about mid to late April, when it joins other such heirloom onions as James Long Keeping, Bedfordshire Champion, Giant Zittau and Long Red Florence.

The time spent in the Melon House in the early part of the season is not without anxiety. Growing row upon row of onions in a humid environment can lead to problems with mildew and, in particular, with aphids. All of Sylvia's workforce have to keep an eye out for early-

season pest outbreaks, especially in such a controlled environment. A strong hatch of aphids could soon rampage through the crop, so if any appear they are mercilessly rubbed out, by sliding thumb and forefinger up the length of the onion stem where the greenfly collect. Despite the fact that all the glasshouses at Heligan are routinely sterilized every winter, and scrubbed down and whitewashed, these procedures will not stop pest problems. Some species are so canny, the slightest nook may hold something undesirable. One of the worst is perhaps the mealy bug, who surrounds himself in a protective wrapping of cotton wool and is very hard to extinguish and very easy to spread around. The stripping of the bark of vines in winter is one means of pest control, especially if there is warmth in the glasshouse during those months.

The onion bed is last year's legume patch. It has had natural nitrogen from the beans and, if time, tide and wind are favourable, it will have been covered all winter by seaweed. The soil is rich, perfumed and back at full fitness after four years of continual cropping.

THE ONIONS IN THEIR ROWS MAKE AN EXTRAORDINARY SIGHT, *above*. THE SMALLEST ONES HAVE JUST BEEN PLANTED AND WATERED IN. STRING LINE, TAPE MEASURE AND WALKING BOARDS ARE ALL CLEARLY VISIBLE.

Shallots are made for stringing, *right*. Much smaller than onions, they fit together perfectly, especially in the hands of Clive, who has made this task his own. Some will make it to the harvest festival at the tea room and the rest will continue to adorn the lean-to in the melon yard.

It receives only a light forking over before being graded for onion planting; and Charles, who does a lot of this forking up, will tell you it is a joy to work. Preceding the onions, the shallots go in and, before them, the garlic will have been planted, after being raised over the winter in the cold frames. The final effect makes quite a sight: row upon row of large single stems, with small multi-headed plants and tiny singles, all at neat regular spaces.

The Victorian method of preparing for the planting of onions was slightly different. In autumn the ground was covered with well-rotted manure. This was forked in and the ground left for the weather to break it down. Rather than being graded to a fine tilth with rakes, any remaining clumps of soil were bashed with the back of a spade or, in Cornwall, a shovel, until the ground was ready for transplanting the onions.

Not long after the onions, the leeks, autumn and winter, are planted. The autumn leeks are raised in boxes from seed sown as early as February and planted out in May. The winter leeks are raised in the time-honoured tradition, in a seedbed in the miscellaneous section of the Vegetable Garden. At about half-pencil thickness they are ready for lifting and transplanting. But because this will happen some time in late June, perhaps the busiest part of the year, the reality is that they will only be moved when there is time available.

Planting leeks is a specialized procedure, in so far as it is designed to blanch the stem in a similar manner to celery, asparagus and chicory. As much light as possible should be kept from the lower part of the plant. Rather than a hole being dug, for each plant an indentation is

JEREMY PEDERSEN DIBS IN LEEKS, *left*. THEY HAVE BEEN TOPPED AND TAILED IN THE MANNER THAT IT HAS ALWAYS BEEN DONE IN ORDER TO SAVE MOISTURE AND MINIMIZE THE STRESS TO THE PLANTS. THEY WILL BE WATERED IN AND THE SOIL WILL FILL IN AROUND THE ROOTS.

Baked Spanish Onions

Ingredients:
4 or 5 Spanish onions.
Salt and water.

Put the onions, with their skins on, into a saucepan of boiling water slightly salted, and let them boil quickly for an hour. Then take them out, wipe them thoroughly, wrap each one in a piece of paper separately, and bake them in a moderate oven for 2 hours or longer, should the onions be very large. They may be served in their skins and eaten with a piece of cold butter and a seasoning of pepper and salt; or they may be peeled, and a good brown gravy poured over them.

ONIONS WE CANNOT, OF COURSE, DO WITHOUT, AND IT IS NO ACCIDENT THAT A FINE COLLECTION OF VICTORIAN VARIETIES HAS BEEN BUILT UP OVER THE YEARS. I AM NO JUDGE OF FLAVOUR BUT I KNOW THAT I HAVE A SOFT SPOT FOR RED ONIONS, AND I ABSOLUTELY ADORE SHALLOTS, ESPECIALLY FOR THEIR USE IN DELICIOUS SAUCES LIKE BEARNAISE.

made, or 'dibbed', in the soil, using a 'dibber'. Some years ago, in a memorable moment of Heligan Vegetable Garden history, Kathy Cartwright commissioned one of the craftsmen on site to make a brass-shod dibber. This is the ultimate in personalized hand tools; Mike Rundle does not like anyone else to use his Cornish shovel because, he maintains, it alters its shape, but even this is outclassed by a brass shod dibber made specifically for leeks. The dibber is easily the best tool for the job, which is to drive a smooth-sided hole 10–15 centimetres into the ground, ready for a single leek plant to be dropped into it. The principle of this is that the deeper the hole the more of the plant is deprived of light, leading to the whitest possible length of shank and therefore the sweetest flesh.

These four essential annual rotations, potatoes and greens as one, followed by roots, legumes and then alliums, were how things started when the restoration of the productive gardens began in 1993. Because the Flower Garden was completely unrestored at the time any semi-ornamental plants were grown in the Vegetable Garden. Eventually, under the description of 'Miscellaneous', these became a rotation in their own right. It was among such oddments that squashes, courgettes and pumpkins were included. In no time the outsize pumpkins and strange-shaped squashes had acquired a fan club. As the area under cultivation in the Vegetable Garden extended, there became room for the fifth rotation, that of the cucurbits: the family of pumpkins and squashes.

PUMPKINS AND SQUASHES

Cucurbit is the fancy name for those members of the plant family Cucurbitaceae which include pumpkins, squashes, melons and cucumbers, and which have come to play an important role in the Vegetable Garden. The cultivation of pumpkins, and winter and summer squashes, which now make up the fifth course of the rotation scheme, is beneficial for two reasons. Firstly, in the climate of Cornwall pumpkins and squashes are not troubled by any particular pest or disease, apart from slugs. This means that there is at least one course of the rotation

ANNIE DIGS SUMMER LEEKS, *above*. THE DYING FOLIAGE OF THE ONION CROP IS EVIDENT ACROSS THE GREEN TOPS OF THE LEEKS AS SHE DIGS THEM OUT WITH A LONG-HANDLED GARDEN FORK IN THE WARM LATE SUMMER SUNSHINE. PREPARED AND READY FOR THE TEA ROOM, *left*, THE LEEKS HAVE MOST OF THEIR ROOTS AND ALL BUT A FEW CENTIMETRES OF THEIR TOPS REMOVED. THE KITCHEN STAFF WILL DO THE REST DEPENDING ON HOW GREEN THEY WANT THE LEEK SOUP TO BE.

free from any build up of a problem which might then overwinter and come back to menace the following season's crop. Their main enemies are cool temperatures at the beginning of the season and frost at the end of it. Secondly, since the plants require significant levels of nutrition to give of their best, plenty of well-rotted horse manure is added at planting. Such a feeding routine can only benefit the soil.

These wonderful plants, so diverse in the size, colour and shape of their fruits, have become very popular with visitors because of the show they put on. This attraction has been brought together as part of a 'Harvest Festival' of Heligan produce, which takes place in the covered area by the entrance to the garden each autumn half term. The stars of the show are without any doubt the pumpkins. Enormous pinkish orange fruits of Atlantic Giant vie for pride of place with the metre-long

green and curly Tromboncino, while the space between them is scattered with Baby Bears and Sweet Dumplings. Further colour is produced by chrysanthemums such as Bronze Elegance and Nantyderry Sunshine. These grow in long rows in the Vegetable Garden as part of the sixth and final rotation, known as 'Miscellaneous'. Even entire plants of mature green curly kale have been known to be dug up, potted up and exhibited. Showing them all off like this is a tremendous way of getting people closer in sympathy to plants.

The popularity of the cucurbits is not limited to visitors; the staff also like them. For one thing they are a low-maintenance crop. Once planted, they need little attention, apart from weeding the 'pumpkin patch', until the rampant trailing foliage, a trait of most varieties apart from the accustomed 'bush' types, takes over and the ground becomes covered in greenery.

The other reason for their popularity with the staff is that they provoke an astonishing amount of praise and wonderment among the visitors. It is hard at first to appreciate the details of what is happening in the patch itself, because the fruits are buried amongst the foliage; but when cooler autumn temperatures arrive and begin to reduce the leaves, this part of the garden takes on the picture-postcard, end-of-season appearance that one comes to expect from pumpkins. Their appearance is even better when they have been carted off and stored under the lean-to in the Melon Yard, next to the Potting Shed. Here they look superb and every day the air is filled with the clicking of camera shutters and the murmured praise of visitors. It is then, with admiration in full supply, that Haydn, Annie, Mike, Clive and Charles can explain that there is no real secret to the growing of these wonderful fruits, great or small, except for the Vegetable Garden's very fertile and healthy soil as provided and cared for by them. By the time they start describing just how much manure they have to barrow around to get such results, the place whiffs of pathos and people start backing down.

Of course there is more to it than that. The routine of caring for the cucurbits as they make their journey from seed packet to Vegetable Garden is a precise one and littered with potential hazards. Timing and patience have a lot to do with eventual success. The trick is for Sylvia to decide exactly when it is best to sow the seed. Too early, and seedlings may have to wait overly long on account of cold weather before they can be planted out. They could become too leggy and in need of potting on, which would waste time, resources, and space in

PUMPKINS AND SQUASHES COME IN ALL SHAPES AND SIZES, *opposite*, BUT AS YOUNG PLANTS THEY ARE REMARKABLY SIMILAR. THERE ARE MANY VARIETIES AND EACH MUST BE INDIVIDUALLY LABELLED, *below*, AS THEY ARE CONSTANTLY BEING MOVED IN AND OUT OF THE MELON HOUSE AND THE COLD FRAMES, *bottom*, UNTIL THEY FINALLY FIND THEIR WAY TO THE SOIL OF THE VEGETABLE GARDEN.

THE FINAL ANALYSIS. AN AWESOME
COLLECTION OF FRUITS, *above*
AND *left*, NO TWO THE SAME, PROMPTED
THE START OF THE AUTUMN HARVEST
FESTIVAL. IT IS A CELEBRATION OF
THE RICHNESS OF THE TIME OF YEAR,
THE GATHERING IN OF THE YEAR'S
PRODUCE, AND NOTHING ACCENTUATES
THAT MORE THAN THE CUCURBITS.
A VICTORIAN GARDENER GLANCING
FROM THE FRUIT STORE MAY HAVE
ADMIRED THIS SCENE.

THE DRAWINGS, *below,* INDICATE THE DEPTH OF VARIETY OF PUMPKINS AND SQUASHES AVAILABLE TO THE VICTORIANS. IT IS A GOOD FAMILY TO GARDEN WITH: OBLIGING, FAST-GROWING AND RELATIVELY FREE FROM PESTS AND DISEASE PROBLEMS, AND SUITED TO OUR TEMPERATE CLIMATE. THE INTRODUCTION OF THIS FAMILY ON A LARGE SCALE TO HELIGAN HAS BEEN A GREAT SUCCESS.

the cold frame. Too late, and the plants would never make up enough time to produce proper-sized fruits. The latter is almost guaranteed never to happen but it must still be taken into account in the successful growing of outdoor cucurbits.

Sylvia sows the pumpkin and squash seeds on edge, rather than flat, in individual seven-centimetre pots of peat-free compost. If they were to be sown flat, this would increase the chance of water gathering around the geminating seeds, with the result that anaerobic respiration might start them rotting. After germination and growth, through the cotyledon up to the true leaf stage, once their roots have filled the seven-centimetre containers the plants are transplanted into one-litre pots. As soon as the weather is warm and the plants have begun rooting into their litre pots, they are placed into the bottom cold frame of the line of three in the Melon Yard. This is where the critical process of hardening off begins and where Sylvia has to decide at what rate this should happen in order to time the plants' arrival in the Vegetable Garden. To begin with she closes the cold frames each night, and opens them in the day only when the temperature is warm. If it is cold and wet the plants are merely ventilated, by the frames being opened a crack. If all this endeavour sounds neurotic, it isn't – on the other hand, the cucurbits are. They are super-sensitive in a way that means they simply will not thrive if asked to cope with low temperatures and cold soil. Once they are planted out it is of course late, but until that time they need and respond to fostering and careful handling. Sylvia is known for her patience and timing, and in return the planting-out date will make itself known to her.

With plants spaced at about a metre from each other, the pumpkin

patch is not double dug in its entirety, because this would be a waste of time, energy and manure. The roots of each plant simply would not reach out far enough into the surrounding space. At planting a hole is dug for each seedling. The hole is then laced with a couple of shovelfuls of manure, which will in fact be more than adequate. Once the plant is firmed in, the soil around its stem is raised up to form a little hillock. This is to support the brittle, fibrous stem and will encourage the plant, as cucurbits are inclined to do, to root further up the stem. Then the plants are watered, and everyone's fingers are firmly crossed in the hope of warm weather undisturbed by any form of sudden and extreme change, because it is now that the cucurbits are at their most vulnerable. With a few days of sun safely gone by, and some warm nights, Sylvia and her gardeners can sleep easy, knowing that they have done everything possible to give the cucurbits in their charge the very best chance.

CUCUMBERS, *above*, HAVE BEEN A REVELATION OVER THE YEARS. THE ALL-FEMALE HYBRIDS JUST KEEP ON FRUITING AND FRUITING WITHOUT FAIL. AS LONG AS THE RED SPIDER MITE IS KEPT AT BAY BY DAMP CONDITIONS IN THE GREENHOUSE ALMOST NOTHING WILL PREVENT THEM FROM PRODUCING A HEAVY CROP. THE BED OF MANURE AND LOAM IN WHICH THEY GROW IS ALMOST CERTAINLY SIMILAR TO THE MANNER IN WHICH THEY WERE GROWN IN 1860 AND THE HIGH NITROGEN CONTENT OF THE SOIL SUITS THEM WELL.

Fried Cucumbers

Ingredients:
2 or 3 cucumbers.
Pepper and salt to taste.
Flour.
Oil or butter.

Mode. Pare the cucumbers and cut them into slices of an equal thickness, commencing to slice from the thick, and not the stalk end of the cucumber. Wipe the slices dry with a cloth, dredge them with flour and put them into a pan of boiling oil or butter; keep turning them about until brown; lift them out of the pan, let them drain and serve, piled lightly in a dish. These will be found a great improvement to rump-steak; they should be placed on a dish with the steak on the top.

I AM PASSIONATE ABOUT CUCUMBERS AND HAVE EATEN THEM EVERY WAY EXCEPT FRIED. ON THE RAILWAYS IN INDIA, WHEN IT IS ESPECIALLY HOT IN SUMMER, THE PLATFORM VENDORS SELL PEELED CUCUMBERS WITH A SMALL PARCEL OF NEWSPAPER CONTAINING SALT MIXED WITH CHILLI POWDER AS THE DIP. DIVINE.

MISCELLANEOUS

This is perhaps an odd title for a cycle in a system of rotation which in some form or other has been practised since crop-growing began, but in the case of Heligan it is an apt description nonetheless.

The Victorians experimented constantly with new species of fruit and vegetable, and with cultivars of those same species. Along the way they also discovered new types of edible crops. From 1993 onwards, as the Vegetable Garden came back into production, space was needed for the Heligan gardeners to find a comprehensive way of reviving this tradition. In fact before alliums and cucurbits each had an entire rotation course of their own, the miscellaneous section was already the fourth part of the cycle. As well as exotics, including the strange root crops Oca de Perou and the Chinese artichoke, there was a place for what might be seen as more conventional crops such as cauliflowers and summer cabbages. These would have been an essential part of the nineteenth-century diet. Salad was included to some extent at that time, but greens were considered indispensable.

If the thinking behind rotation is founded on moving crops around the garden in their families, the Miscellaneous section defies all the laws. Here are to be seen strange brassicas such as the swollen-stemmed Kohl Rabi, and the strong-scented, bulbous-rooted celeriac. Celery, celeriac, extra salad potatoes for which room could not be found in the main potato section, even seedbeds for winter leeks and biennial flowers – they all find their way into the Miscellaneous section and it is here that some solid horticulture is learned.

For old-timers such as Mike Rundle, who was farm-born and bred, sowing leeks or winter brassicas in a seedbed for transplanting has been part of a normal routine. But for today's horticulturist fresh from college the days of seedbeds are over. Now the brassicas at Heligan are pot-raised, although Annie and Haydn can still be found in midsummer sowing winter leeks in seedbeds. The wallflowers and sweet Williams that fill the beds either side of the apple arch with colour, and the air with scent, also start life in a seedbed. This dying practice gives the gardeners a strong sense of authentic achievement. By contrast with raising the young plants under glass, they have so much less control over conditions outside and to succeed on such terms feels to them like proper gardening.

Consider it this way: your task is to produce an awe-inspiring summer bedding display of the biennial sweet William. The space to fill is roughly 45 square metres, running half the length of the Vegetable

CHINESE ARTICHOKES, *top*, AND KOHL RABI, *above*, ARE TWO OF A LESSER KNOWN GROUP OF VEGETABLES THAT WERE FAR BETTER KNOWN ONE HUNDRED YEARS AGO. KOHL RABI HAS ALWAYS BEEN EXCEPTIONALLY POPULAR IN GERMANY, WHILE THE CHINESE ARTICHOKE, LARGELY BECAUSE OF ITS FIDDLINESS, NEVER QUITE MEASURED UP TO THE HEAVY-BEARING JERUSALEM ARTICHOKE.

Garden next to the apple arch. This is a prime site, open to admiration – or dissatisfaction – from those in any position of greater responsibility. All you have at your disposal is no more seed than you should need and a short row of bare ground in the Vegetable Garden to use as a seedbed in which to raise the plants. From sowing to blooming the time allotted is eleven months.

Open-ground sowing at any time is a big risk, of that there is never a doubt. Perfect sowing conditions one July day – warm damp soil – can be followed by a torrential downpour the next, scattering seed and soil everywhere. Once Annie has chosen what seems a good day for sowing, the ground will be lightly forked over and graded to a level surface and the seedbed then marked out with a string line. The fine-tooth landscape rake is then brought into action, to create that small crumb-like structure required for a seedbed, which is known as a 'fine tilth'. Then a 'drill' is taken out in the soil with the tip of a trowel, and the seeds sown in the bottom of the drill about half a centimetre apart. The row is then firmed in by hand and watered.

Assuming no monsoon arrives, germination will follow; but it may be erratic – small stones can trap seed, air may be squeezed out, tiny insects can eat emerging cotyledons – there are no end of hazards. Assuming too that a relatively even rate of germination is achieved, the next task is to monitor growth until some thinning out may be necessary. With leeks this does not usually happen except at the transplanting stage, when the choice is made of which seedling to use and which to discard. But with sweet Williams you have more of a plant, by which I mean more stem and more leaves which need to have developed properly to be considered for transplanting. Always at the back of Annie's mind is that, since the sweet Williams are not for eating in winter, they have to hold the ground, staying there through the seasonal hazards of weather and pests and then produce fabulous blooms in the following summer. It is a tall order and therefore selection is crucial.

The demands laid upon a head gardener to balance the garden's different elements in Victorian times were considerable, and they remain so today. Experience and craft were essential to the disciplines

THE LONG STEMS OF ANTIRRHINUMS, *left,* ARE ONE OF THE GREAT TALKING POINTS OF SUMMER IN THE VEGETABLE GARDEN. THE OLD VARIETIES GROW FIVE TIMES TALLER THAN ANY OTHERS AND MAKE A FANTASTIC DISPLAY. PRECISION IS FOUND ALL OVER HELIGAN: THE CLEAN LINES OF THE FLOWER GARDEN, *below,* CONTRAST WELL WITH THE HAPHAZARD GROWTH OF THE ANCIENT RHODODENDRONS WHICH HANG INNOCENTLY OVER THE WALLS. *Overleaf,* THE VEGETABLE GARDEN.

required in growing hugely diverse ranges of fruit, vegetables and flowers. However, as McIntosh pointed out in the Preface to the *New and Improved Practical Gardener*, such knowledge was indeed available. It was understood therefore that for someone in the position of head gardener at a garden of national importance such as Heligan, the relevant skills would duly be in place.

COMPOSTING

Composting has always been a very important aspect of horticulture, and it has never been more closely valued and researched than today. Recycling is part of our lives and all of us are, or should be, aware of the wasteful throwaway culture in which we live. Within the horticultural industry, the use of peat is finally being seen as hard to justify, considering that it is almost a finite resource. As such, it needs to be replaced by other forms of compost.

Recycling has always been a part of gardening, with nutrients being constantly replaced throughout the garden in the form of compost. Ideally no components from outside are used, so that self-sufficiency is the norm in every department, and gardeners can be confident in the quality of their materials.

The amount of organic matter required in the Vegetable Garden is immense. With arable crops the average need for farmyard manure is ten tons per acre; it follows that at least the same, if not more, is used up in both the Vegetable Garden and the Flower Garden. Taking into account the Pineapple Pit's additional need for a considerable amount through the winter, it is possible to build up a picture of quite how much muck has to be heaved around the gardens.

Almost everything of an organic nature that is unwanted in the two productive gardens – every weed, every rotten apple and every part of every spent plant – finds its way onto the compost heap. Once there it will break down, to be returned to the soil where it can release its carefully stored stock of nutrients.

The critical thing to help the process on its way is

to add small amounts at a time and to make sure the pieces themselves are small. The breakdown process requires an even distribution of air and water to allow the fungi, the bacteria and all the other organisms that contribute to the breakdown of the organic matter to do their job.

Sylvia and Helen know this perfectly well, and a visit to either of their compost heaps will reveal all waste matter either chopped or broken up into small pieces. Grass cuttings, supplied by James Hyland from the Sundial Garden, are spread evenly over the heap rather than being dumped in a lump, and thick brassica stumps are either smashed up or carted away for burning. The ash from the fire in the Head Gardener's Office is added by Clive Mildenhall to the compost heap in the Flower Garden as a valuable source of potash, which of all the major nutrients is the most soluble in water.

Formerly the compost might have been used for the propagation of plants. Now, however, it is dug into the ground whenever there is a shortage of farmyard manure. It is also used as a mulch, although there can be a problem with weeds germinating if the heap has not heated up enough to kill off their seeds.

The heaps are never turned, so that in the course of three months during the warmer times of year a full heap will have cooked and produced the best quality of compost imaginable. Once the individual heaps in the productive gardens are full to bursting, their overspill is taken to the new works area, where a series of industrial-sized compost bays have been built. This is where any surplus materials, such as topsoil, extra compost and the incoming farmyard manure, are stored.

For all the emphasis we put today on composting, it is interesting to note that in Victorian horticulture composting was practised largely for the production of soil for plants grown in containers. Most fresh green matter from the garden, such as weeds, or spent haulm from potatoes or peas and beans, was laid in a trench dug into the garden and had soil thrown on top.

PESTS AND DISEASES

The management of pest and disease problems throughout the garden has two sides: the traditional and the bang up to date. There are so many things which can go wrong in any case that, generally, potential problems in the garden must be anticipated and looked at long before they actually appear. One example is the wire netting that encircles the outside of the Vegetable Garden to guard against rabbits; likewise the

THE GIANT OAK, *above,* AND THE BANKS OF CORNISH RED RHODODENDRONS, *left,* PROVIDE AN UNUSUAL BACKDROP TO THE VEGETABLE GARDEN. COLOURFUL AND STATUESQUE, THEY MAKE THE JOB OF WORKING THE GARDENS YEAR ROUND A PURE PLEASURE. BIOLOGICAL CONTROLS, *below,* HAVE BECOME A VITAL WEAPON IN THE ARSENAL FOR CROP PROTECTION. GIVEN OPTIMUM CONDITIONS THEY ARE EXTREMELY EFFECTIVE AND CAN GREATLY REDUCE THE POPULATION OF CERTAIN PESTS.

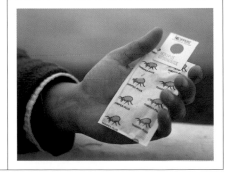

practice of covering the brassicas in the Vegetable Garden with netting as a preventative measure against the wood pigeons that would otherwise feed on several kinds of crop. Throughout the estate similar types of precaution are taken; for example in the form of tree guards against livestock and deer, and humane traps for smaller kinds of animal.

It is always preferable to be working towards prevention rather than the cure. If you are seeking a cure it can only mean there is an existing problem. Perversely, though, in state-of-the-art pest and disease control as practised in areas of protected cropping, such as glasshouses and polythene tunnels, the problem must exist before it can be cured.

Throughout the natural world, biological controls are the simple order of play: one insect to kill another. Similarly, with a pest problem in a glasshouse it is a matter of introducing a controlling insect to kill that pest. The difficulty is that the population of that pest must achieve a given size if the controlling insect is to thrive. Timing of the latter's introduction is critical and Sylvia, Mary and Steve now have this down to a fine art. When biological control works it is super-efficient. But, if

DIVIDE AND RULE, *left*. FIRST KEEP THE AERIAL THREAT AT BAY AND SECOND THE ONE FROM UNDERGROUND. WOOD PIGEONS ARE A MENACE AND ALTHOUGH THEY FAVOUR BRASSICAS THE BROAD BEANS ARE NOT EXEMPT FROM THEIR ATTENTION. ROOKS AND JACKDAWS ARE ALSO PARTIAL TO THEIR TENDER, JUICY YOUNG SHOOTS SO THE PLANTS ARE COVERED WITH NETS THROUGH THE WINTER AND INTO THE EARLY SPRING. MICE CAN APPEAR FROM ANYWHERE AND THESE HUMANE TRAPS ARE EFFICIENT AND KIND, THE MICE BEING RELEASED SOME DISTANCE AWAY. OTHER PESTS: THE JERUSALEM ARTICHOKE APHID, *above*, AND THE APPLE SAWFLY AND GRUB, *opposite*.

not, it is a huge waste of money because on any terms it is expensive.

Before there were modern means of prevention against pests, or new cures in the shape of biological controls, the art of horticulture, then as now, boasted skilled gardeners and high standards. In 1820, for example, the work of wily gamekeepers did much to make up for the absence of wire netting.

Although some aspects of horticulture can be complex, the real secret of producing healthy plants is to know and understand their everyday requirements, in particular their preferred soil type and growing conditions. At a very basic level if you give a plant food, water, light and air you can expect that plant to grow. If you give it a healthy soil, by and large you will produce a healthy plant. Everything the plant gets is from the soil; this is the foremost point to understand about horticulture. At Heligan, where Philip has led by example, his insistence on the rotation scheme in the productive gardens has proved to gardener and visitor alike that this is how it works in gardening: without healthy living soil the required results will not be achieved.

This does not mean you will never see another slug in your garden; it means instead that where there is health, the plants are less likely to have poor resistance to pests and diseases. Close observation is also needed, along with an understanding of whether any particular problem is due to the climate or to any other cause beyond the gardener's control. Not only did the Victorians know that healthy soil was the critical starting point from which to grow disease- and pest-resistant plants; they appreciated that close day-to-day supervision was also vital to this end. It was in Victorian times that entomology became widely recognized as a help to horticulturists. In books and periodicals, gardeners were encouraged to start collections of injurious insects, and to study their habits from the egg onwards. The collection of slugs by hand, though primitive, was nonetheless considered to be a very effective method; and in fact this is still the most common form of reducing their number, alongside the use of the slug nematode as a biological control. Nineteenth-century gardeners were encouraged to pinch out the tops of any plants under attack from aphids, and tobacco was regularly used to defumigate glasshouses. Lime was also used, to spray against pests, and crop coverings were in constant use to keep birds away. The use of the hand-held net exercised very good control of the cabbage white butterfly. No doubt this task was carried out by the small boys who were probably also employed in scaring birds away and clearing the Vegetable Garden of stones.

3 FRUIT

Growing fruit, the experts say, is very difficult in Cornwall. Even George Gilbert, former fruit officer at RHS Wisley and a veteran of the Long Ashton Research Centre, would shake his head sadly when talking of trying to grow tree fruit in this county. A Cornishman himself, for the last few years George has been advising on fruit cultivation at Heligan, where he has been only too aware of the poor light levels that prevail, along with the great variety of fungal diseases caused by the Duchy's perennially damp conditions.

GEORGE GILBERT AND SYLVIA TRAVERS INSPECT THE WALL FRUIT AT HELIGAN, *right*. ONE OF THE MOST COMPLICATED AND IN-DEPTH OF ALL HORTICULTURAL TRADITIONS, THE TRAINING OF FRUIT TREES TO WALLS, FENCES OR STRUCTURES OF ANY KIND TAKES SOME LEARNING. YOU ONLY GET ONE CHANCE WITH THE SECATEURS; ONE WRONG MOVE CAN COST YEARS. *Opposite*, THE APPLE ARCH IN THE VEGETABLE GARDEN HAS REACHED MATURITY AND ABUNDANCE WITHOUT TOO MANY SCARES.

Every time George has come for a visit he has left perplexed at how well everything was growing and how the disasters forecast by him had failed to show. This too is attributable to that extreme carefulness, with nothing left to chance, which is such a prominent feature of working methods in the gardens at Heligan. I once had the honour of working for the great racehorse trainer Vincent O'Brien. So determined was he to train Derby winners that he built a gallop identical to the Derby course at Epsom. Result: six Derby winners. The same attention to detail can be seen in the way Sylvia addresses herself to cultivating the various wall fruit: a supreme example of this meticulous mindset.

The work involved in growing wall fruit is still enormously labour intensive, even with the help of the horizontal wires against which the trees are trained. Wire was not invented until the late Victorian era; before that, the branches of the trees were held in place by a system known as nailing and tagging. This involved banging a nail into the wall and tying the branch or shoot to the nail with a strip of cloth left over from the local tailor's shop. This system was used for training ornamental climbers as well as fruit trees, which left pockmarked walls throughout the garden. These marks are perhaps as much a signature of Heligan's Victorian past as even the Glasshouses, the boiler rooms and the Pineapple Pit.

PINEAPPLES

In Victorian times the demand for fruit from the garden would have been high, just as it was for other produce. Strenuous demands were put upon the gardening staff and the head gardener in particular. But with new varieties coming to their attention all the time, those who were quick learners had plenty of chances to trial the most recent arrivals and put their own growing skills to the test. With the backing of a rich patron great results could be achieved and nowhere was this more so than in the growing of pineapples.

The reconstruction at Heligan of the giant frame designed by the Victorians solely for cultivating pineapples was at the core of the restoration project in the mid-1990s. As the team responsible for this rebuilt and restocked it, the horticultural fame of Heligan was established once more and travelled far and wide. As an indication of how seriously the cultivation of this fruit was taken in the nineteenth century, whole classes were designated for pineapples at horticultural shows of the time. Victorian horticultural books were filled with all possible information on 'pines'. McIntosh, in 1843, has whole chapters devoted to raising pines and even to the construction of the pine house.

The cultivation of pineapples today at Heligan barcly differs from that of a hundred and twenty years ago. The Pineapple Pit comprises a large frame covered by 'lights', which are in effect windows in the same vein as those that cover cold frames. It is confusing that the construction and the covering are both called frames. The pit acts as the growing chamber and it is here, under the cover of the lights, that the pineapples grow. The plants are produced in pots which in turn are 'plunged' into a bed of leaf mould.

There are two major differences in the cultivation of today and that of the Victorian era. Firstly, no longer is there a hot water system running underneath the pit to provide bottom heat; and secondly, there is no fermenting tan bark available in which to plunge the pots of pines. In the early years of re-establishing pineapple production, trips were made to the tannery in Grampound, not five miles from Heligan, to collect the oak bark used there for tanning leather. However, this never heated up, and my suspicion was that the bark had done its fermenting by the time we collected it. It was either that, or the difference made by a lack of underground heating.

Either side of the growing chamber are the manure pits. This is where the real fermenting takes place. Horse manure has always been the dung of choice, as it would have been under the Victorians, largely

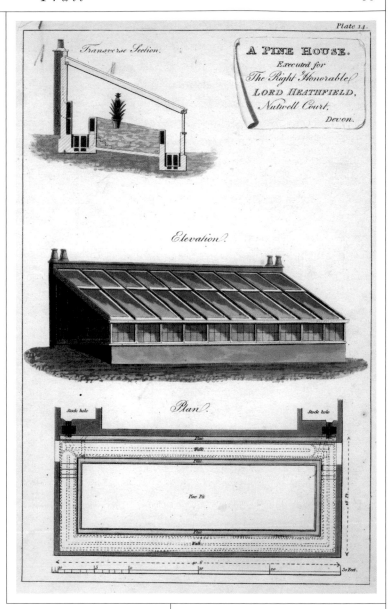

ALL CANES AND NO FRUIT. A FAN-TRAINED APRICOT ON THE CURVED WALL OF THE MELON YARD, *opposite*. THE ANGLE IRONS WHICH SUPPORT THE HORIZONTAL WIRES CAN CLEARLY BE SEEN. IN THE EARLY YEARS THE BRANCHES OF THE TREES ARE TIED TO CANES. IT IS ESPECIALLY GRATIFYING WHEN THE TREE TAKES OVER FROM THE CANES. *Above,* A PINE HOUSE WAS A VERY GROWN UP VERSION OF THE PINE PIT.

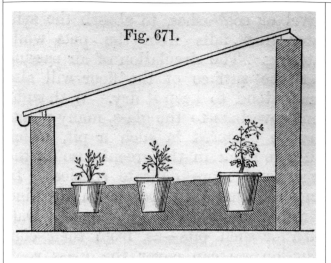

Fig. 671.

PLUNGING THE POTS OF THE PINES IN SUITABLY WARM AND FERMENTING MATERIAL SUCH AS TAN BARK, *above*, WAS CONSIDERED AN IMPORTANT PART OF CULTIVATION. WHEN ALL GOES TO PLAN THE RESULTS ARE MAGNIFICENT, *right*: A SMOOTH CAYENNE PINEAPPLE.

because the stuff was so abundant. However, not any old manure will do. It has to be of a strawy consistency and must have a high concentration of nitrogen, provided in the form of urine. This, along with the muck itself, aids the bacterial and fungal activity that creates the necessary heat. The heap, when it arrives from the stables, has to be turned by hand at least twice before the right degree of heat is attained. Only then can it be transferred into the pits. When fermenting does begin, the heat is intense and before now I have been able to pick cooked if extremely pungent carrots out of the heap.

From the pits the heat permeates the sides of the frame and passes into the growing chamber via the walls. These are constructed of honeycomb brickwork, which is constructed with spaces between each brick to let the heat through. This process happens three times a year, in autumn, winter and spring. The labour and technical skill involved is immense but the rewards are also huge. There is almost a sense of occasion in the way that Mike, Clive and Charles heave the manure into the pits both front and back; it is a communal task that involves a lot of staff and though the work is gruelling it is carried out with a great sense of pride.

The cultivation of the pineapple plants is the responsibility of Sylvia. She has her own specialized potting mixes and feeding regimes, but the make-up of the soil in the pots consists largely of a light loam (John Innes no.3), some grit and a little charcoal, while the feed is mostly seaweed and liquid manure, applied once a week in summer when the plants are in good growth.

The great enemy of the pineapple is too much wet. As with all bromeliads the plants like water through the centre, or crown, but in winter problems can arise through condensation. If the weather is too cold to allow ventilation, condensation can build up on the undersides of the lights and drip down on to the plants. At this time of year the plants are somewhat dormant, so that excess moisture is not taken up and they can start to rot. This is why it is critical to procure large amounts of fermenting manure through the year. So often in the climate of Cornwall it is the case that the enemy of growing exotic plants under glass is too much moisture rather than too much cold.

The pineapples growing at Heligan today are direct descendants of several original suckers that arrived from South Africa on the Bank

Preserved Pineapple

Ingredients:
To every lb. of fruit, weighed after being pared, allow 1 lb. of loaf sugar; ¼ pint of water.

The pines for making this preserve should be perfectly sound but ripe. Cut them into rather thick slices, as the fruit shrinks very much in the boiling. Pare off the rind carefully, that none of the pine be wasted; and, in doing so, notch it in and out, as the edge cannot be smoothly cut without great waste. Dissolve a portion of the sugar in a preserving-pan with ¼ pint of water; when this is melted, gradually add the remainder of the sugar, and boil it until it forms a clear syrup, skimming well. As soon as this is the case, put in the pieces of pine, and boil well for at least ½ hour, or until it looks nearly transparent. Put it into pots, cover down when cold, and store away in a dry place.

IMAGINE THE LUXURY OF BEING ABLE TO TAKE BASKETS OF RIPE PINEAPPLES INTO HELIGAN HOUSE IN THE NINETEENTH CENTURY — A SEEMINGLY EXOTIC IDEA, YET FOR A PERIOD IT WAS THE NORM. IN 1997 THE FIRST CROP OF PINEAPPLES AFTER THE RESTORATION OF THE PINEAPPLE PIT ARRIVED AND IT WAS A BIG ONE. IT HAS BEEN AN AMAZING ACHIEVEMENT TO GROW PINEAPPLES AND GREAT FUN AT THE SAME TIME.

Holiday Monday of May 1994. The varieties are Smooth Cayenne (a joy to handle on account of the absence of spines on the leaves) and Queen, very prickly but handsome nonetheless. Both fruit well and are still in rude health, the experiment having been a huge success after the steepest possible learning curve. It is a fine moment indeed when Sylvia puts out the word that she has harvested a ripe pine and that a tasting session is on the go.

STRAWBERRIES

The three cold frames in the Melon Yard, lined up across the path from the Pineapple Pit, each have their own purpose. The bottom one is for hardening off plants destined for the Vegetable Garden, while the top two alternate between being used for raising strawberries and for growing cucurbits, in the form of cucumbers and melons.

The joy of picking and eating a sun-warmed strawberry when the frames are opened first thing on a late June morning is another special detail that puts the gardeners at Heligan in a privileged position. But again, achieving this is not easy. Strawberries are notorious for their susceptibility to botrytis, and Sylvia has to use all her skill to prevent the build-up of this fruit-spoiling fungus, all the while clambering in and out of the frames, gently moving from one walking board to another so as not to compact the soil.

The variety of strawberry grown at Heligan is Royal Sovereign. Old-established and with a delicate skin, which became superseded by tougher varieties, it nonetheless has a flavour beyond compare and is one of the few period-correct varieties still available. The plants are mulched around with straw to protect the ripening fruit from soil splash, which can also encourage fungal spores, and to discourage slugs, which are not keen on clambering over the sharp, crispy ends of wheat or barley straw.

At the end of the strawberry season, as the leaves are beginning to get somewhat tattered and the plant has taken back enough energy into the crown, Haydn or Annie will once again climb back into the frame and cut off all the runners and most of the foliage. This will reduce the chance of red spider

YOUNG FIG TREES IN POTS, *below*. FIG CULTIVATION AT HELIGAN HAS ALWAYS BEEN A TOPIC FOR DISCUSSION. THE OLD BROWN TURKEY FIG, AN ORIGINAL PLANT FOUND DURING THE EARLY YEARS OF THE RESTORATION, WHICH RESIDES IN THE BACKGROUND AGAINST THE WHITEWASHED WALL OF WHAT WAS PROBABLY ONCE ITS ITS VERY OWN FIG HOUSE, IS CRYING OUT TO BE REPLACED. YOUNG PLANTS IN TUBS LOOK GOOD BUT REMAINING OUTSIDE ALL WINTER DOES NOT ALLOW THEM TO RETAIN THEIR FRUIT THROUGH THE SEASON.

mite or aphids overwintering in the frame, and at the same time it will reduce the likely number of slugs and snails. The frames are then taken off for the autumn and winter, so that the plants can go properly dormant and form fruit buds, and are stacked neatly under the lean-to by the Potting Shed in the corner of the Melon Yard.

The third and final cold frame is shared between cucumber varieties such as Crystal Apple, Crystal Lemon, and Bedfordshire Prize Ridge, and watermelons. These are allowed to sprawl across the soil, where Sylvia can pretty much leave them to themselves.

WALL FRUIT

Heligan has always set its gardeners a challenge, whether it is to grow pineapples in the nineteenth-century fashion or to clear the steep sides of the Jungle. To grow fruit against walls is a complex business and one of the hardest areas of productive horticulture in which to succeed consistently.

Establishing the trees, especially against walls or fences, is everything, so it is important to give them optimum conditions in which to succeed. Pruning can be studied and learned but the first essential cuts in the early years of a fruit tree's life are crucial. Sylvia, to whom this responsibility falls, has learned well. It is easy to rush and even

CUCUMBERS 'CRYSTAL APPLE' AND 'CRYSTAL LEMON', *above*, ARE GROWN IN ONE OF THE THREE COLD FRAMES FOUND IN THE MELON YARD. ALONGSIDE ARE A COLLECTION OF KNIVES PROVING THAT NOT MUCH HAS CHANGED IN THE DESIGN OF PRUNING, GRAFTING AND GENERAL PURPOSE KNIVES.

panic. This is not the way; once you make the cut there is no going back. Sylvia's practised technique, and her confidence in her own ability, has made her an expert, with the trees and their harvest there to prove it.

If the trees are growing strongly and the pruning is done correctly, all that cannot be relied upon is the weather. Favourable conditions at pollination time are particularly important. What a sight the apple arch makes that runs from north to south down the central axis of the Vegetable Garden when in full flower during the spring. Laden with blossom, it is a magnet for bees on a still, calm, sunny day and it is these conditions that guarantee good pollination. Yet all can be spoiled, by one late frost that sits down on the blossom and ruins all the good work of the bees. It is rare that frost can be late enough to cause damage to the crop, but it is not impossible.

The arch is not made up, as many people imagine, of indigenous Cornish varieties. Rather, it comprises varieties of apple which might have been cultivated in Cornwall in the nineteenth century.

THE HOOPS OF THE APPLE ARCH IN HIGH SUMMER ARE PICKED OUT BY THE ANTIRRHINUMS IN FULL FLOWER, *below*. THE LATER SEASON ASTERS ARE PICTURED IN THE FOREGROUND ALONG SIDE THE BOX HEDGING. THEY WILL GIVE CONTINUITY OF COLOUR THROUGH THE LATE SUMMER AND INTO AUTUMN.

ONE OF THE TWO CORNISH APPLE
ORCHARDS FOUND AT HELIGAN,
left, THIS ONE SLOPING DOWNHILL
BEHIND OLD WOOD. THE VARIETIES
ARE ALL INDIGENOUS, UNLIKE THOSE
TREES IN THE APPLE ARCH IN THE
VEGETABLE GARDEN, WHICH ARE
PERIOD-CORRECT BUT ARE NOT
SPECIFICALLY CORNISH. THE APPLE
ARCH, *below.*

They include such delights as Laxton's Epicure, The Reverend W. Wilkes, Ellison's Orange and the splendid dual-purpose Lord Derby.

The Cornish varieties are grown at Heligan in two orchards. One is sited between Shepherd's Barn and the Stewardry and is also home to the collection of poultry, as well it might have been in the Victorian era. The other is on the north side of Old Wood next to the Wildlife Project.

The orchard trees are grown on the most vigorous rootstock, M25, as Philip believes this places much less stress on the trees than if they were grafted on to more dwarfing stock. This in turn lessens the likelihood of disease that threatens apples in Cornwall and is why Cornish varieties were developed in the first place. Since disease can get in through pruning cuts (as with silver leaf on prunus species), as a double safeguard against scab, and canker in particular, the trees are never pruned. The collection of trees is primarily about building up disease-free stock for future propagation. Consequently it is of little concern that leaving the trees unpruned may lessen the crop. Meanwhile this enables them to develop in their own way and to grow as they would have been allowed to one hundred and fifty years ago. The grass underneath is kept cut, and staking ensures support.

Apple Fritters

Ingredients:
For the batter, ½ lb. of flour, ½ oz. of butter, melted to a cream, ½ saltspoonful of salt, 2 eggs, milk.
Apples.
Hot lard or clarified beef-dripping.
The flavour of the fritters would be very much improved by soaking the pieces of apple in a little wine, mixed with sugar and lemon-juice.

Break the eggs; separate the whites from the yolks, and beat them separately. Put the flour into a basin, stir in the butter; add the salt, and moisten with sufficient warm milk to make a batter that will drop from the spoon. Stir well, and add the whites of the eggs, which have been previously well whisked; beat up the batter for a few minutes. Now peel and cut the apples into rather thick whole slices and stamp out the middle of each slice with a cutter. Throw the slices into the batter; have ready a pan of boiling lard or clarified dripping; take out the pieces one by one, put them into the hot lard, and fry a nice brown, turning them. When done, lay them on blotting-paper before the fire; then dish on a white doyley, piled one above the other; strew over them pounded sugar.

There is nothing quite so comforting as cooked apples. A dish of stewed apple, warm with sugar and Cornish cream can be as good as a pudding gets. Heligan is short on cooking apples apart from the two orchards filled with the Cornish varieties. Many of them are cider varieties and they are almost all inedible raw, so the pot is the place for them.

Although the apple arch cannot strictly be described as an example of wall fruit, the trees are trained to make an arch, and it is this discipline that demands the greatest skill. There are only three branches on these trees: one central stem and, protruding from this, two horizontal branches just above the box hedging that runs the full length of the garden. Again, this offers little or no margin for error.

The north wall of the Melon Yard is where most of the wall fruit can be found. On its south- and west-facing sides there are cordon-trained (single-stemmed) and espalier-trained apples and pears, as well as fan-trained apricots, cherries and plums. On the Vegetable Garden side there are also fan-trained plums and a large Morello cherry. Loganberries have also been trained against this wall. By way of a neat extra touch, by the archway into the Melon Yard from the Vegetable Garden there are also some cordon-trained redcurrants.

As support for all these fruits, their individual shoots are tied to long bamboo canes. These in turn are fastened to horizontal wires

SYLVIA TIES IN A FAN-TRAINED PLUM ON THE NORTH-FACING WALL OF THE VEGETABLE GARDEN. ENORMOUSLY LABOUR-INTENSIVE, IT IS A JOB THAT HAS TO BE CARRIED OUT AT KEY MOMENTS OTHERWISE THE PROGRESSION IS LOST AND CONFUSION WILL TAKE OVER. THE OPEN CENTRE OF THE OLD-FASHIONED FAN-TRAINED TREE IS CLEARLY VISIBLE: ALL THE LATERALS APPEAR FROM THE TWO FORKED BRANCHES OF THE 'Y'. THE BLOOM ON A RIPENING PEAR, *right,* IS A JOY TO BEHOLD. THE APPLE SAWFLY, *above.*

STRAWBERRIES, *above* AND *opposite*, COMMAND A LOT OF RESPECT FROM ALL QUARTERS. WHEN WELL GROWN THEY CROP HEAVILY. THE RAIN IS THE ENEMY, BRINGING FUNGAL PROBLEMS WITH IT FROM SOIL-SPLASH ON TO THE FRUIT. IT IS A CONSTANT BATTLE TO KEEP THE PROBLEMS AWAY AND IN A RAINY SEASON THE HUMIDITY BENEATH THE LEAVES AND AROUND THE FRUIT DOES NOT HELP.

which are held in place by strong upright angle irons. The organisation of these plants is a fruit fancier's dream. It looks perfect, and deserves the fullest admiration.

SOFT FRUIT

As well as strawberries in the cold frame, there is also a large bed of Royal Sovereign strawberries in the Vegetable Garden. As with the plants in the frames these demand a lot of work throughout the season. In such a fertile soil they are bound to grow vigorously and from mid-summer onwards Annie or Haydn may have to de-runner them as much as twice. The extra work is not seen as a hardship though, because by mid-July the harvest they produce will be extraordinary, and achieving it is one of the great treats of working in the Vegetable Garden.

There is also good a collection of bush fruit. These take some careful winter pruning to keep them bearing strongly, and again, along with a fine collection of cordon gooseberries, this is Sylvia's responsibility. But all the gardeners learn to keep an eye out for anything unusual, and with bush fruits there is an enemy which, if not caught in time, can cause havoc. The sawfly's little devil of a striped caterpillar can strip a bush of its foliage in a few days and, because it hides on the underside of the leaves, the gardeners have to be on alert, through June in particular, to watch for any hatches. So much of horticulture is observation, as Heligan's gardeners, under the guidance of Philip and Sylvia, know well, to the point where it can soon become second nature.

ROYAL SOVEREIGN, *below*, IS UNMISTAKABLE DUE TO ITS PALE COLOUR AND CLOSE-KNIT SEEDS ON THE SKIN. A VERITABLE PRINCE AMONGST STRAWBERRIES.

4 GLASSHOUSE FRUIT

There are four glasshouses in which fruit is grown at Heligan. The Melon House produces both melons and cucumbers, the double Paxtonian Vinery grows dessert grapes, the Citrus House is home to the orange and lemon trees during the long winter months and the Peach House provides nectarines and peaches. All of these crops are tricky; I would go so far as to say that growing fruit under glass in the 'old-fashioned' way is the hardest bit of traditional horticulture — at least it was for me when I began learning — although somehow Sylvia Travers, whose responsibility it is to produce the highest standard of fruit, makes it look easy.

A CORNER OF THE PEACH HOUSE, *above,* WHICH OCCUPIES ALMOST ALL OF THE SOUTH-FACING WALL OF THE FLOWER GARDEN, PEEKS OUT OVER THE COMPARTMENTS OF BOX HEDGING. *Right,* GLASSHOUSES FOR QUEEN VICTORIA, PROBABLY BY FOSTER & PEARSON OF NOTTINGHAM-SHIRE WHO BEGAN DESIGNING AND BUILDING GLASSHOUSES IN 1841.

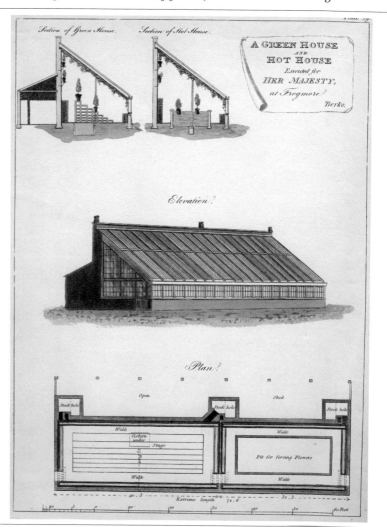

More pages in practical horticultural books are given over to this matter than any other; more thought has to go into individual pruning cuts, more care into temperature control, watering, pest and disease problems, ventilation and so on. It is akin to a military campaign in the Napoleonic Wars — everything has to be accounted for from the moment the plants awake from their winter dormancy to the time the leaves fall and sleep comes again. Between times victory must be won at all costs.

There is still a connection today, in my mind, with the nineteenth century when everything was so very formal, particularly in the garden. Matching the expectations of the past doubles the importance of getting the job done well and heightens the satisfaction when results exceed expectation. Today, praise for a fantastic crop of peaches flies

A SELECTION OF SOME OF THE TOMATOES, SWEET PEPPERS, CHILLIES AND AUBERGINES, *above*, THAT GROW IN POTS IN THE CITRUS HOUSE ONCE THE CITRUS HAS BEEN MOVED OUT ON TO THE TERRACE FOR THE SUMMER.

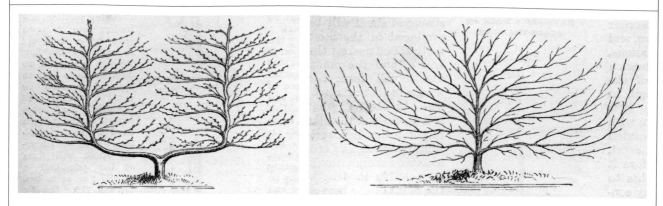

about like confetti from all and sundry; two hundred years ago mild praise for a job well done, but expected to be well done, might have been about the limit.

PEACHES

As the peaches are grown today in the manner it is assumed they were grown two hundred years ago, in a glasshouse rebuilt to the same specifications as the original one and on the same site, it is academic whether praise is forthcoming or not.

Of all the fruit mentioned above peaches are probably the least troublesome for, in my opinion, they offer the best return. They grow all over the south of France, Italy and the United States, where they are the fourth most important commercial crop after apples, oranges and grapes, having started life in China where they were first cultivated at least

THE TRAINING OF PEACHES IN VICTORIAN TIMES, TO DEVELOP A STRONG TREE FRAMEWORK TO SUPPORT THE WEIGHT OF THE FRUIT, AND TO OPEN UP THE TREE CANOPY TO MAXIMISE LIGHT PENETRATION, WAS THE SUBJECT OF MUCH EXPERIMENTATION, *above* AND *left*. THE GREATEST SKILL OF ALL IN GROWING PEACHES COMES IN THE TRAINING AND PRUNING OF THE TREES. THE PROGRAMME OF SEASONAL WORK CARRIED OUT AT HELIGAN IS HIGHLY SKILLED AND INTENSIVE AND REQUIRES MINUTE ATTENTION TO DETAIL.

THERE ARE ALSO TREES PLANTED ON THE BACK WALL OF THE GLASS-HOUSE, *below,* ALTHOUGH STRICTLY SPEAKING THEY ARE MISPLACED, SUFFERING AS THEY DO FROM THE SHADE CAST BY THE TREES IN FRONT.

three thousand years ago. By putting a glasshouse over them we are simply duplicating the hot summers of their native habitats. Conversely, in the winter, peaches need a period of cold treatment to allow them to go properly dormant in order to set fruit buds: therefore all the ventilation, doors and windows stay wide open through November and December to let the cold air in.

The training of the trees to suit the glasshouse is the hardest bit but, like a lot of the technical side of horticulture, once you understand the principles the process quickly becomes straightforward.

Heligan bends the rules slightly in that there are peaches trained as

espaliers rather than fans. This is a hard discipline because peaches fruit on one-year-old wood and on an espalier this is usually to be found further and further along the branch year after year. The branches of fans can be placed and tied wherever there is a gap and this makes life much easier.

Artificial heat is not required in any peach house and the soil that was present in the Flower Garden on the exact same site as the original Peach House has barely been altered save for the introduction of some organic matter at planting. Feeding is restricted to a mulch in the summer months and watering is done thoroughly once a fortnight, although Sylvia takes care to damp the soil down daily through the season and syringe the plants with water to keep the red spider mite at bay. Pest and disease control is a serious concern and comes in the form of 'biological controls'. A year-round plan is in operation to deal with scale insects, mealy bug, red spider mite and aphids.

Harvesting is done when and only when the smell of ripe peaches in the glasshouse is so heady and overpowering that the fruit could not be anything other than ripe. Gentle pressure applied to the fruit will lead to bruising and blemishes if the fruit is not fully ripe so this must be avoided. The temptation of visitors to squeeze the fruit — 'just to see' — has proved too much on occasions.

The joy of a glasshouse provided solely for the production of peaches is almost a dream of extravagance, so it is good that there are incidental advantages to be had from this luxury. The glass protects the peach leaf from curl fungus and lessens the possibility of attack from another fungus, silver leaf, which comes in through wounds or pruning cuts when the spores are active during the winter months. To avoid attack from silver leaf, those members of the Rosaceae family which carry stones, such as peaches, nectarines, plums, cherries and apricots, must only ever be pruned in the summer.

The greatest skill of all when cultivating peaches comes in the training and pruning of the trees. The planting of the young trees at the front of the glasshouse, 30 centimetres in from the brick base on which the sloping glass rests, may seem unusual in that the plants are then trained up at a 45-degree angle underneath the glass, but this was the former way and so faith is kept with this tradition. A system of evenly spaced horizontal wires runs the full length of the glasshouse and to this all the shoots are tied. There are also trees planted on the back wall of the glasshouse although strictly speaking they are misplaced, suffering as they do from the shade cast by the trees at the front.

ALTHOUGH PEACHES ARE SELF-FERTILE THEY BENEFIT GREATLY FROM A LITTLE AID IN THE POLLINATION DEPARTMENT. THEY FLOWER EARLY IN THE SPRING, *opposite,* WHEN THE GLASSHOUSE IS SHUT AGAINST FROST AND FEW POLLINATING INSECTS CAN GET IN – IF THEY ARE EVEN STIRRING AT ALL. WHEN THE POLLEN IS RIPE AND GOLDEN, SYLVIA WILL BRUSH EACH FLOWER WITH A RABBIT'S TAIL ON A STICK OR A PLAIN AND SIMPLE PAINTBRUSH.

T HE RESULTING CROPS OF PEACHES
ARE OFTEN HEAVY, *above,* AND
FRUIT THINNING HAS TO TAKE PLACE
DESPITE THE NATURAL FRUIT DROP.
YET STILL, SOMEHOW, THERE ONLY
EVER APPEARS TO BE A MARKED FALL
IN PRODUCTION WHEN IT COMES TO
DISTRIBUTION. PERKS OF THE TRADE
PERHAPS!

The purpose of planting and training directly beneath the glass is to allow the trees the benefit of maximum light and warmth.

In the south of England it is perfectly possible for peaches to be grown outside against south-facing walls or fences. For anyone planning to attempt this it is worth pointing out one aspect apt to be overlooked in modern cultivation of fan-trained trees. Partly trained trees are sometimes available from nurseries. But for the tree to be correctly shaped you must make sure that all the shoots are growing out from two original laterals, or side shoots, which are trained at about 40 degrees from the main stem and are not protruding up it continuously.

The programme of seasonal work carried out by Sylvia on the peaches is intensive and highly skilled, requiring minute attention to detail. Depending on the weather the season starts early, perhaps even at the end of February when the blossom, borne on bare wood, starts to appear. Peaches are self-fertile but hand pollination, done only when the pollen is golden and therefore ripe, will improve cropping. To transfer pollen from the anthers of one flower to the stigmas of the other, a fine-haired brush or rabbit's tail is used.

This is a seminal moment in more senses than one, being among the most significant operations to be carried out so early in the year. It heralds things to come: there are few sights more extraordinary than the Peach House on a sunny day in early March filled with a mass of pink flowers from which in summer a heavy crop of luscious fruit will appear.

Following on from pollination, leaves start to appear, then tiny fruits. Disbudding must be done, to prevent too many of next year's shoots from flowering; and soon it is time to thin the fruit so as not to overburden the tree. The shoots are further thinned, and those due to fruit next year are tied in. The harvest follows, after which fruited wood is removed in favour of young shoots to provide next year's crop. To produce a properly trained tree which fruits well year after year is a highly skilled task and one that takes all the meticulous devotion of a true gardener.

Of the varieties grown in the Peach House most plaudits must

Compote of Peaches

Ingredients:
1 pint of syrup.
About 15 small peaches.
Syrup: To every lb. of sugar
 allow 1 ½ pint of water.

To make the syrup: boil the sugar and water together for ¼ hour, carefully removing the scum as it rises: the syrup is then ready for the fruit.

Peaches that are not very large, and that would not look well for dessert, answer very nicely for a compote. Divide the peaches, take out the stones, and pare the fruit; make a syrup, put in the peaches, and stew them gently for about 10 minutes. Take them out without breaking, arrange them on a glass dish, boil the syrup for 2 or 3 minutes, let it cool, pour it over the fruit, and, when cold, it will be ready for table.

IT IS ONLY WHEN THERE IS A GLUT AND ONE OR TWO ARE BRUISED AND BEGINNING TO BROWN THAT THE MOMENT ARRIVES TO THINK ABOUT COOKING PEACHES. THIS HAPPENS MOST YEARS, AND THERE ARE VERY OFTEN WINDFALLS SUCH IS THE QUANTITY. WHAT A LUXURY — A BAKED PEACH IS A WONDERFUL TREAT.

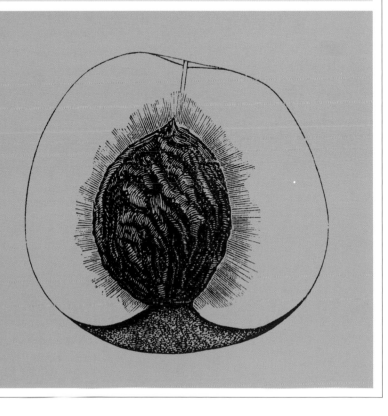

THE VICTORIANS WERE NOT AFRAID TO EXPERIMENT WITH UNUSUAL TRAINING STYLES FOR FRUIT TREES, *below.* IN THE TYPES OF GARDENS WHERE FRUIT WAS GROWN IN QUANTITY THERE WAS NOT ONLY THE TIME AND THE MONEY BUT THE SKILLED LABOUR TO DO THE WORK. THE DESSERT GRAPES IN THE PAXTONIAN DOUBLE VINERY, *opposite,* ARE NOT GROWN IN ANY FANCY MANNER; RATHER THEY GROW ON SINGLE 'RODS' IN THE MANNER OF A CORDON.

surely go to the white-fleshed variety known as Peregrine. The yellows Rochester and Duke of York are no lesser fruits, but white flesh is unusual in the modern day, and the flavour is quite exceptional. Freshness for consumption is essential — slightly more so with the whites as they do seem to bruise that bit more easily. Nonetheless there is no shortage of takers for a warm, ripe peach picked straight from the tree on a July morning.

GRAPES

The Flower Garden holds two other glasshouses as well as the Peach House. This intimate walled garden, has a central dipping pool for watering, and beds crammed with early summer vegetables and annual and perennial flowers for cutting. In addition, tucked away in the southern corner is a large fruit house which has appropriated the name of the Citrus House. Adjoining it is a splendid double Vinery which is home to a period-correct collection of dessert grapes. If ripe peaches taste blissful, then the chance to devour a freshly picked bunch of ripe Black Hamburgh grapes must come a close second.

The double Vinery is to the design of Sir Joseph Paxton MP, former head gardener to the Duke of Devonshire at Chatsworth in Derbyshire and designer of the Crystal Palace for the Great Exhibition of 1851. Paxton was a remarkable man who rose from a simple background to become one of a number of men and women who shaped the face of English horticulture throughout the nineteenth century. What was particularly extraordinary about Paxton in the context of this Vinery

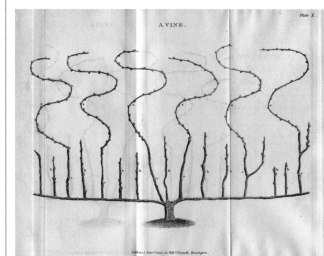

is that he had developed a buy-to-order system whereby the purchaser could order a glasshouse to arrive at the delivery address in sections, to be assembled and glazed by the estate workers. The individual sections of Heligan's Vinery are clearly visible, as the glasshouse was rebuilt to the original template taken by John Nelson in 1995.

While the Peach House is virtually true to its original purpose and the peaches themselves are grown in the traditional way, in the system of cultivation within the Vinery there are two major differences from the past.

To begin with, the heating system is defunct. This is not so serious today, when we have only

THERE CAN BE FEW GREATER
LUXURIES THAN HOME GROWN
GRAPES FROM ONE'S OWN GLASSHOUSE,
above. BUT BY ANY STANDARDS IT IS
A JOB THAT DEMANDS GREAT SKILL.
CLIMATE, IN PARTICULAR THE FALLING
TEMPERATURES AND LIGHT LEVELS
IN THE AUTUMN WHEN DESSERT
GRAPES ARE TRYING TO RIPEN, PLAYS
A BIG PART.

ourselves to please with the quality of dessert grapes produced. But it certainly would have been in the late nineteenth century, when Squire Tremayne's expectation of the highest-quality fruit for his table was paramount.

All the workings of this system nonetheless remain visible. The hollow wall in which, before the advent of solid fuel boilers, fires were lit to produce heat, still makes up the back of the glasshouse. Adjoining the Head Gardener's Office behind the Vinery is the old boiler house, featuring the solid-fuel Britannia boiler which later pushed hot water around the cast iron pipes; these too are still in evidence in the Vinery today.

The other missing link is the outdoor bed to the front of the glasshouse, in which the original vines would have been planted. A brick terrace now lies here, on which many thousands of pairs of feet tread each year. This is in contrast with some other gardens; visitors to the great vine at Hampton Court Palace, for example, will have seen that over an enormous area outside the Vinery there is bare soil on which it is prohibited to walk because this is the ground into which the great vine's roots have spread.

According to the old-fashioned way, vines were planted outside the glasshouse and each plant fed through a semicircular hole in the wall at or just above soil level and into the house itself.

When the cultivation of dessert grapes began again at Heligan the vines were planted inside the house due to uncertainty about what might become of the area outside. As it was, in 2002, after eight years of successful growth and fruiting, the vines died, following an attack from an obscure fungal disease called Eutypa, which typically affects vines grown under glass. On digging out the soil to try and discover the source of this problem it became clear that at a certain depth the soil inside the glasshouse was unsuitable. The closeness of the terracing outside the Vinery would have made no difference.

The dead plants were removed and a fresh start made, this time using topsoil from the Vegetable Garden, with home-made compost. Starting vines from scratch is a precarious enterprise. The plants arrive from the nursery as mere twigs, less than a metre high and looking very delicate. Even so, the stem is then cut back at planting to two buds,

THINNING OF THE FRUIT WITH IMPLEMENTS SUCH AS THESE, *below*, IS ANOTHER VITAL PART OF SUCCESSFUL DESSERT GRAPE PRODUCTION. IN PARTICULAR IT HELPS TO STAVE OFF THE FUNGAL DISEASES WHICH CAN RUIN THE CROP WHEN ALL THE FRUIT IS BUNCHED TIGHTLY TOGETHER. IT TAKES FOREVER AND IS AGONY ON THE ARMS BUT IF IT CAN BE ACHIEVED WITH THE BLOOM LEFT INTACT ON THE FRUIT IT IS A JOB WELL DONE.

leaving no more than perhaps 15 centimetres of wood sticking up from the ground. For anyone starting out with vines it is inspiring to think that from those two buds will emerge a vine which, if it equals the Hampton Court vine, will produce grapes for centuries.

For the first two years the aim is to get the main stem or 'rod' growing strongly and vertically, as it is from this that the side shoots or laterals originate which produce the fruit. The vine must be prevented from flowering during this time so that it can strengthen before putting its energy into fruit production.

In the spring of the third year after planting, the vine begins to grow in what will be its first fruiting season. It seems implausible that the tiny, upside-down, already cone-shaped flower heads could possibly turn into bunches of grapes. They look so insubstantial and, unlike members of the Rosaceae family such as peaches and apples, which produce one fruit from one bloom, vines produce a ready-made bunch of grapes from each cluster of flowers.

Hardly has pollination taken place, aided by Sylvia gently running both hands once down the bunch of flowers, than the fruit will set and

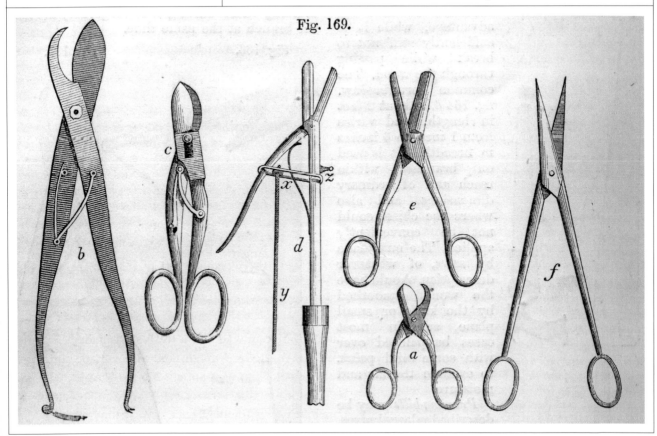

Fig. 169.

THE VINERIES ARE ALSO HOME TO A NUMBER OF DECORATIVE PLANTS IN POTS AS THE CLIVIA, *below,* AND *Fothergilla major, opposite,* BEAR WITNESS. HELIGAN HAS BEEN COLLECTING PLANTS THAT WOULD HAVE BEEN A BIG PART OF DECORATIVE VICTORIAN HORTICULTURE SINCE THE START OF THE RESTORATION. THESE INCLUDE A LOT OF BULBOUS PLANTS SUCH AS GLADIOLI, IXIA AND NERINE WHICH PHILIP MCMILLAN BROWSE LEARNED TO GROW WHEN HE WAS GROWING UP ON THE ISLES OF SCILLY.

thinning must be done. This is the secret of perfect bunches of grapes, especially in cold glasshouses. As the night-time temperatures drop when the bunches are ripening in the early autumn, the lack of warmth provokes the onset of fungal diseases. Proper thinning lessens the chance of this setback, by allowing free movement of air in and around the immature grapes.

Standing on a ladder, neck arched, grape scissors and forked stick in hand, anyone thinning grapes is truly removed to a bygone era. The grapes must not be fingered on any account as this may spoil the bloom; the stick is there to turn the bunches as they are thinned. It is virtually only in the glasshouses of the great gardens that tasks such as these are carried out. Those who do such work know themselves to be exceptional. Once it was part of each season throughout many gardens; now it is restricted to a handful.

As the grapes swell through the summer, a careful watch must be kept for pests and diseases. Just as with peaches, grapes suffer from such typical glasshouse pests as red spider mite, mealy bug and white fly, so further biological controls must be in place to deal with these.

Meanwhile a mulch of horse manure around the base of the vines retains moisture and adds nutrition, and watering is done only when the soil surface is seen to be drying out. The true level of moisture content is discerned by drilling a hand-held augur into the soil. It is essential to find out how much moisture is present around the roots which can grow to a depth of up to 60 centimetres.

The moment of harvest is a landmark in the year, and once word of it gets around the staff crib room it is certain that such a sought-after crop will not last long. This was not the case when grapes were being produced for the house. Then, the crop had to be staggered and fresh bunches were required at a moment's notice. Unlike peaches, which do not keep well and should be eaten as soon as possible, with grapes there is a way to store the fruit and maintain freshness. It entails cutting the bunch to leave as much stem as possible; the stem is then inserted into a bottle filled with water which has a few lumps of charcoal in the bottom. Wine bottles will serve and should be fixed at a 45-degree angle so that the bunch hangs free. A cool, frost-free shed should be

Aubergines, *above,* have a pleasing habit of coming out in all different shapes of sizes, but they are not that easy to grow, having minds of their own about how they want to perform. When they get it right they are spectacular and full of flavour.

chosen for this type of storage, with the less moisture in the air the better.

It is convenient that the Vinery at Heligan is in two sections. Being adjacent, they allow for a succession of grapes, from the earliest ripeners such as the sweetwater Chasselas Rose, which has the most delicate pink grapes, up to the late-maturing varieties including Lady Downe's seedling, whose huge great purple berries fill the mouth with juice. In between come such favourites as Black Hamburgh and Muscat Hamburgh, this last with the tell-tale flavour of muscat — the real signature of home-grown grapes.

After harvest and leaf fall, two more horticultural tasks take place in the Vinery that are rarely seen elsewhere. Firstly the loose bark of the rods is removed. This practice is as hazardous as it sounds — if live bark were removed, the vine could die. The purpose is to remove pests, in particular mealy bug, which may be lurking beneath any spontaneously lifting bark.

The second job is to lower the rods, to allow bud formation evenly up the stem. The sight of these bare cordon vines suspended at chest height is a strange one: for the month of December each rod is untied from the horizontal wires which hold it in place and lowered to a 90-degree angle. But once this essential task is done it can be safely said that the vines have been put to bed for the winter.

CITRUS

The love affair of English gardeners with citrus is enormous; so too the general desire to grow citrus trees at home. Sylvia will tell you that one of the most frequently asked questions is, 'How do you get your citrus looking so good?' The answer she supplies is, 'Don't overwater and don't overfeed' — these being the two main reasons why most people's citrus plants underperform.

The citrus trees at Heligan are planted in Versailles boxes, in free-

A SMALL AUBERGINE, WHITE EGG, *above*, IS A JAPANESE VARIETY WHICH EVENTUALLY TURNS YELLOW WHEN FULLY RIPE. THE PLANTS GROW IN LARGE TERRACOTTA POTS, ONE PLANT PER POT, AND RESIDE IN THE CITRUS HOUSE AFTER THE BIG PLANTS ARE MOVED OUT ON TO THE TERRACE.

A GLASSHOUSE IN WHICH LARGE CITRUS TREES CAN HIDE DURING THE WINTER, *below,* IS THE PERFECT PLACE. THE PLANTS LIKE TO BE DRY AND COOL; THEY ARE OFTEN KILLED WITH KINDNESS BY BEING GIVEN TOO MUCH WATER AND TOO MUCH HEAT. THEY LIKE TO BE TREATED ROUGHLY: EXCESS WATER AND THEY WILL DROWN, HIGH HEAT AND THERE WILL BE A POPULATION EXPLOSION OF APHIDS. *Opposite,* SUMMER ON THE TERRACE AND AN ABUNDANT CROP.

draining compost with plenty of added grit. From October they spend the winter in the Citrus House and go out at Easter to pass the summer on the terrace in front. This suits them very well, and the greatest joy besides their excellent quality of fruit is the fact that they produce both sweet-smelling blossom and fruit at the same time and throughout the year.

Their roots are necessarily restricted by the boxes, and in summer unless there is rain they have to be watered about once a week. In winter they need watering probably once a month and then only when the top few centimetres of compost have dried out. They are fed in summer once a fortnight with a 50:50 mix of liquid horse manure and liquid seaweed; and each winter the top couple of centimetres of compost is scraped away and replaced with new. Pruning is done in the winter months, to shape the tree in the manner required.

The control of pests and diseases is paramount. As with the other three glasshouse crops, peaches, grapes and melons, any build-up of pests can be rapid, so Sylvia spends a considerable amount of time on biological controls and on checking for infestations. Because the

THE MEXICAN NATIONAL COLOURS IN HOT CHILLIES, *right*. THEY HAVE BEEN STRUNG TOGETHER BY SYLVIA FOR THE AUTUMN HARVEST FESTIVAL. GROWN IN THE CITRUS HOUSE ALONG WITH THE AUBERGINES AND THE TOMATOES THEY ARE A WHIMSY THAT ALLOWS THE GARDENERS TO TEST THEIR SKILLS.

greenhouses are unheated, it is too cold in the winter for many of the insect-eating predators to live, so extra vigilance is needed to forestall any outbreaks of the often hardier pests. In Cornwall's mild winter climate there is little slowdown in the breeding rate of pests such as aphids. These are particularly noticeable on the young growth of citrus trees and have to be squashed by hand or sprayed with soft soap. Scale insects can quickly take a hold and these have to be scraped off, while the woolly down which hides the dreaded mealy bug can be penetrated with methylated spirits.

MELONS

The Melon House, a pretty glasshouse in the Melon Yard, which adjoins the Vegetable Garden at Heligan, may perhaps claim more atmosphere and history than any other corner of these great gardens.

It was the first of the glasshouses to be rebuilt, even before anyone knew whether the restoration project had enough behind it to do anything with the Flower Garden. At the time of the resurgence of this curved walled garden, in early 1994, every other undertaking seemed a long way off. The Melon House, along with the Potting Shed in the corner of the yard, became a sanctuary for the gardeners. Here everything was propagated that had to be started from seed and it was here that the history of the pineapples began when they were delivered from South Africa.

Classified as a three-quarter-span house, it is the oldest glasshouse in the garden, possibly dating from as early as 1820. It is divided into three sections, which over the course of 2004 were completely rebuilt by Adrian Burrows and his estate staff.

The two larger sections, which have open raised beds, are used for growing melons and cucumbers in alternate years. Each one is divided, their soil being changed annually, and both crops have a section every year to themselves.

The third section of the glasshouse is given over to propagation, and houses a heated frame where seeds are started off. In place of a solid-fuel boiler, the remains of which are still visible in a dark hole behind the glasshouse, the Melon House now has electric cables placed under the huge slabs of Delabole slate which make up the bases of the raised beds. This helps with the progress of the young plants destined for the Vegetable Garden and also provides warmth around the roots of the melons and cucumbers once they have been planted in the soil.

Lemon Wine

Ingredients:
To 4 ½ gallons of water allow
*   the pulp of 50 lemons,*
*   the rind of 25.*
16 lbs. of loaf sugar.
½ oz. of isinglass.
1 bottle of brandy.

Peel and slice the lemons, but use only the rind of 25 of them, and put them into the cold water. Let it stand 8 or 9 days, squeezing the lemons well every day; then strain the water off and put it into a cask with the sugar. Let it work some time, and when it has ceased working, put in the isinglass. Stop the cask down; in about six months put in the brandy and bottle the wine off.

ONE OF THE MOST VERSATILE OF FRUITS. THOUGHT TO HAVE ORIGINATED IN EASTERN ASIA, LEMONS WERE INTRODUCED TO BRITAIN BY THE CRUSADERS AND ARE FIRST RECORDED GROWING IN ENGLAND IN 1577. THE VICTORIANS DREAMED UP ALL KINDS OF WAYS TO USE AND COOK THEM.

The Melon House is a focal point for staff working in the productive gardens, and it may be that the cucumbers and melons get just that extra bit of attention because of the prominent position of the glasshouse. This is as well, because melons are not easy to grow. With cucumbers, the all-female varieties which are grown at Heligan are bullet-proof hybrids with a guaranteed no-bitterness stamp. Melons, on the other hand, can be quite contrary, contracting stem rot and dying at a whim, the slightest nick with secateurs or a knife turning to death and crop failure. It can be a war of nerves with melon plants; it seems they are looking for an excuse to give the grower a hard time.

The flesh of the netted types, so called because of the raised webbing over the fruit, is coloured green, orange or white and are delicious, if only you can bring them to maturity. I have to agree with T. W. Sanders, the doyen of writers on the subject of fruit: 'It requires a good deal of experience to be able to grow melon fruits to perfection … thus, great care is necessary to maintain the plants in a healthy condition until quite ripe.' This is a fair warning, because melons can almost be said to seize on your mistakes and punish the unwitting gardener, especially one that is inexperienced.

The propagation of melons is straightforward, with the seed sown in good compost, on its edge to avoid water collecting around it. The growing on of young plants in the warmth of the glasshouse is also relatively hazard free. Stem rot may arise from the removal of unwanted leaves or from watering too close to the plant, when a simple splash of spore-carrying soil on to the stem may start the problem off. Verticillium wilt can appear for no apparent reason. What makes it hard to grow healthy plants is that the glasshouse needs to be kept humid for the purpose of controlling red spider mite control, and this provides excellent breeding grounds for fungal diseases.

As with peaches the young melon plants are planted against short bamboo canes close to the front wall and about a foot apart. As they grow they are trained underneath the sloping glass to the apex of the house where the glass slopes back down for a few feet before coming to rest on top of the back wall. All the foliage is tied to the wire from underneath. This way the plant is allowed to grow free from hindrance by the wire. It is a very precarious process because the melon plant would really like to creep along the ground rather than climb a set of horizontal wires. If shoots are allowed to bend unnaturally and tissue is broken disease can enter in. To the unfamiliar eye the tangle of undergrowth spewing forth in all directions and dotted with little

THERE IS NOTHING QUITE AS SATISFYING AS A MELON HANGING IN A NET AND QUIETLY RIPENING UP THROUGH THE LATE SUMMER: BLACK ROCK, *left*, AND BLENHEIM ORANGE, *below*, WITH ITS NETTED SKIN.

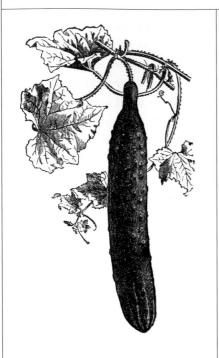

yellow flowers must seem like an unkempt jungle. The reality is that Sylvia knows exactly which shoot belongs to which plant, and where to expect the appearance of each ripening melon gently suspended in its jute string net as summer wears on.

Pollination is done with a rabbit's tail and, once fruits have set, each plant is limited to a maximum of five. It can feel like a long season when growing melons, as you wait for the season when the smell of the ripening fruit begins to fill the glasshouse. A final tally of around forty melons may seem plenty but, for the work that goes into this and the space taken up, by modern standards it is a prodigious luxury; at the time the glasshouse was built it was of course normal. The marvel is that the necessary skills are still intact, and much appreciated by visitors to whom a glasshouse filled with strange-looking balls hanging up in nets is a very odd sight.

CUCUMBERS

We tend to think of cucumbers as vegetables, and we eat them as such; but they are in fact fruits, members of the cucurbit family, which also includes melons as well as squashes and pumpkins.

Compared to melons, cucumbers can look even more impressive as a crop, hanging down from the main stem of each plant. The fruits are produced between each leaf axil, roughly every 23 centimetres. Thus a mature cucumber plant can offer the spectacle of between 10–15 fruits hanging down in varying stages of maturity at any one time.

The relative ease of cultivation of the glasshouse cucumber is for three reasons. One is that they are grown as cordons — single-stemmed plants; this avoids the problem of tangled foliage, unlike melons; instead you have an orderly plant with all the side shoots and tendrils pinched out on appearance, leaving only the fruit hanging down. Secondly, cucumbers are much sturdier than melons, and less prone to fungal problems. Thirdly, the types grown at Heligan are modern all-female hybrids which are failsafe in everything from germination to fruiting to flavour. In this they are unlike the melons cultivated here, which are old varieties such as Hero of Lockinge and Blenheim Orange, and lack the advantages of 'hybrid vigour'.

The concession to modern varieties of hybrid cucumber is one of only a handful made at Heligan. The majority of all vegetables and fruits grown in the productive gardens are chosen only from varieties that were in cultivation before 1910 and therefore likely to have been

The near perfect cucumber crop, *below* and *overleaf,* always invites a lot of interest. The varieties are all female f1 hybrids and as such produce a fruit at every node almost without fail. The result is a heavy crop, and often a second crop through the late summer and autumn. A green giant ridge cucumber, *opposite.*

grown at Heligan during its heyday. In the early days of gardening at Heligan our beautiful crop of Telegraph cucumbers were deemed to be too bitter by Lyn Nelson, John's wife and doyenne of the Tea Room in the early 1990s, so in the following season we changed varieties.

The Melon House stands directly beyond the Pineapple Pit, the spent manure from which goes toward making up the beds in which the melons and cucumbers grow. Having heated the Pineapple Pit through the winter the manure is removed to make the base of the beds, about 15 centimetres deep. A further 20 centimetres of John Innes no.3 compost is added to complete the final mix. From the time of fruit set, liquid seaweed is added weekly to this combination, in which both melons and cucumbers grow very happily.

5 THE FLOWER GARDEN

The Flower Garden, also known as the Walled Garden, has remained true to type since its inception. Odd though it may sound, half the garden is devoted to early summer vegetables; this is on account of its gently sloping southerly aspect. The other half is devoted to annual and perennial flowers, bulbs and sweet peas. There is an extensive collection of herbs, both annual and perennial, and the whole area is divided up by an intricate maze of hedges of box, camphor, escallonia and pomegranate. It is a garden of extremes, hot and stifling when crowded with visitors in summer, and cold and exposed during winter, especially for a walled garden. The range of glasshouses — the double Vinery, the Citrus House and the Peach House — add to these extreme effects. This is particularly so in winter when bare soil abounds, while in summer they reflect light and heat with equal intensity.

HAZEL TWIGS TIED INTO HORIZON-TAL WIRE AWAIT THE ARRIVAL OF THE SWEET PEA PLANTS WHICH ARE PLANTED AT THE FOOT OF THE TWIGS OUT OF PICTURE, *opposite*. THE RHODODENDRONS OUT IN THE BACK-GROUND INDICATE THAT SPRING IS IN FULL SWING AND ANOTHER SEASON IS UNDER WAY. THE FLOWER GARDEN IN ALL ITS GLORY, *following pages*.

The Flower Garden makes a special demand on those who work in it, for the paths are often choked with people asking a seemingly endless series of questions and sometimes it can feel like their interest can displace the actual job of gardening. The garden is worked by a number of part-time staff under the experienced direction of Helen Wilson, for whom no aspect of horticulture, including questioning from visitors, can hold any fear.

A YEAR IN THE LIFE

Apart from its glasshouses, a year in the life of the Flower Garden is much like that of the Vegetable Garden, with its crops of fruit and vegetables growing alongside one another. In other ways, however, it is more complex.

This is largely because the soil in the Flower Garden is only starting out on its journey towards maximum fertility. Already this has taken a lot of effort, since in its original state the quality was very poor. It is hard to know whether this was due to extensive cropping during Heligan's lean years before and after the Second World War, or whether it had only grown cut flowers and had therefore been poor by design. Whatever the reason, the topsoil here has neither the depth nor the richness of colour to be seen in the Vegetable Garden. Certainly the

Flower Garden was still being used as such by the inhabitants of Heligan House long after the Vegetable Garden had fallen into disuse, with the result that its soil was probably being denuded rather than improved.

The pressures on Helen and her helpers can in some ways be tougher than for those who work the big main-crop Vegetable Garden. On the precious piece of ground that slopes downwards from the Peach House, the vegetables grown here are expected to be earlier than the first produce in the Vegetable Garden, and this can often be problematic. Also, this being the Flower Garden, visitors expect to see flowers. However, before they get to the borders in the Sundial Garden, the only ones they will have seen are those on either side of the path in the Vegetable Garden.

As visitor numbers begin to increase throughout the early months of spring and up to Easter there is little colour to be had in the Flower Garden. Nonetheless the bleakest January days, when everything in the Flower Garden seems dormant, are splashed with the unexpected colours of the anemone crop and its strong dark hues of red and blue mixed in with rich pink and creamy white. This spectacle is provided by *Anemone* 'St Piran', one of the earliest flowering of the biennial cut-flower crops. It was through the hot days of late summer that Helen planted the corms yielding her this harvest of colour, and by August her thoughts are already turning to the following season.

Anemones are a very important cut-flower crop within the Cornish industry, not least because they bloom early, when for company they have only daffodils and narcissus. It gives Helen a great feeling of satisfaction to have nursed the plants through the winter, and to produce such a vivid array of flowers both for cutting and for visitors to admire in their beds.

Life starts early too for other biennials in the Flower Garden, in particular ranunculus. Here, though, there are potential problems, for if planted as corms directly in the soil during autumn they can be prone to rotting. Helen starts them in pots and grows them on in cold frames in the Reserve Garden before planting them out in late autumn along with

ANEMONES HAVE ALWAYS BEEN AN IMPORTANT CUT FLOWER CROP IN WINTER IN CORNWALL. THIS VARIETY BEING PICKED BY HELEN WILSON, *below,* IS *Anemone* 'ST PIRAN', NAMED AFTER ONE OF THE MANY PATRON SAINTS OF CORNWALL. WELCOME COLOUR IN THE WINTER, THEY LAST WELL IN WATER AND BRIGHTEN UP THE BARE SOIL OF THE VERY WINTERY FLOWER GARDEN, *opposite.*

the Brompton stocks. The difference with the stocks is that they are grown from seed. They provide early scent and, as spring draws to its close yet still before the first hardy annual crops come into flower, the sharp-coloured pinks, yellows and oranges of the ranunculus are at their sweet-shop best.

Over the winter Clive is called in to help with the digging of the areas of the Flower Garden that need to be double dug. The earliest of the first early potatoes are grown here and, while Mike tends to the seed in store, Clive and Charles barrow down several tons of spent manure from the Pineapple Pit to go into the potato trenches.

Soon after the potatoes are planted, as close as possible to 1 March, it is time for Helen to think about putting out her summer cabbages and cauliflowers. These, like the stocks, she has raised from seed. To cultivate flowers as well as vegetables and herbs, she needs to draw on all her experience and knowledge. It is a huge responsibility, especially when suddenly the season has started and there is no going back. Helen has to juggle with crops as diverse as sweet corn and sweet marjoram; meanwhile everything needs close attention to detail, as well as demanding its own unique approach.

Yet the gardening day begins not with planting or harvesting or any such landmark occupation. For Helen, as for Haydn and Annie in the Vegetable Garden, the first emphasis is on tidying up ready for presenting the garden to the visiting public, and that means raking and sweeping.

The previous day's visitors and the to-ings and fro-ings of the staff have left scuffed paths and unkempt corners, all of which must be made to look pristine. Gardening in the public eye is bound to demand this; so each morning out come the rubber rakes, and every path throughout the garden is given a thorough raking. Leaves are collected and put in leaf-mould bins. This exercise also gives the staff the day's first look at the garden and a chance to notice anything that might have happened overnight and that now needs attention. The brick paths are swept that lead from the Vineries down past the dipping pool where the gardeners used to fill their watering cans, and into the Sundial

Horse manure is turned for the pineapple pit, *above*, before it finds its way to both the vegetable and the flower gardens to be dug into the soil as required by the rotation. The silt and mud that Charles Fleming is digging out of the dipping pool, *top right*, will end up on the compost heap and eventually be returned to the garden, *bottom right*.

Garden. With a start time for the gardeners of eight o'clock, by a quarter to nine the garden looks a picture.

Once the summer brassicas are safely in and protected from a host of potential enemies such as cabbage root fly and wood pigeons, Helen can begin to think of sowing the open-ground crops. These are the varieties of sweet and succulent vegetables that, in direct contrast to the main full-season cropping of the Vegetable Garden, are harvested in succession. Carrots for bunching, beetroot, spring onions, early Milan turnips and radishes are all produced in the two big beds beneath the Peach House, along with the French beans grown for eating rather than drying. The surrounding boxes are planted with sweet corn and quantities of annual herbs such as curly- and flat-leaved parsley, the demand for which is high in the Tea Room.

This is a garden of huge abundance, largely due to its cycles of crop clearance and replanting. Its produce includes plentiful salad crops, in particular lettuce and endive. Faultless production is needed by the trickier varieties such as the giant cos lettuces and the frizzy endive. Having tied up the maturing plants with raffia to keep out the light and thereby blanch and sweeten their centres, Helen knows exactly when to harvest them and send them up to the Tea Room for consumption by the public. There is a fine line between an immaculate creamy yellow head of endive to one which has gone over and started to rot. The first is a delicacy, the second is inedible, the flavour of the whole plant having changed completely.

Watching Helen direct drill her seeds in the open ground is to have the benefit of a master class. The key to all direct drilling is to combine a very fine tilth with a drill that avoids being overly deep. Helen uses the tip of a trowel, moving it back and forth along the row to spread the soil evenly. That done, it is critical to sow the right density of seed. Some gardeners in the productive gardens go to the length of laying down a tape measure along each row, the better to measure out exactly the spacing of the seed. This practice was begun some years ago by Kathy Cartwright and shows the perfect attention to detail which has always been her hallmark. Meanwhile, with the instinct of one who has done this for a very long time, and with a no-nonsense Northern style of self-confidence, Helen sprinkles the seed by sight, trusting herself to judge the quantities that will yield the right amount of seedlings in each row. One object of this exercise is to limit the amount of thinning out that will be needed. In warm weather, when soil temperatures are above ten degrees centigrade, everything will germinate, with the result that oversowing will mean lots of extra thinning out. This is a hard job, which entails donning knee pads, dropping on hands and knees, and removing individual seedlings until the right amount is left at the right spacing in each row. It is murder on the back as anyone will tell you, especially Mike Rundle, who has made an art of thinning the long rows of root crops in the Vegetable Garden.

PRODUCE, LOVELY PRODUCE. THERE IS SO MUCH OF IT ALL THE YEAR ROUND, AND NEVER ANY TROUBLE IN FINDING A HOME FOR IT. ANDREA MURFITT, *above*, WHEELS TWO BOXES OF LETTUCE UP TO THE TEA ROOM WHILE, *opposite*, THE DARK FOLIAGE OF THE BEETROOT 'BULL'S BLOOD' HIDES ONE OF THE BEST VARIETIES OF ALL FOR FLAVOUR. *Previous pages*, THE FLOWER GARDEN IN SUMMER.

FLOWERS

There is a lot to juggle with in the Flower Garden, because while on one side of the garden work goes forward on tasks like picking beans or bunching carrots, on the other there are the flowers to be cared for. After the biennials, in the form of anemones, Brompton stocks and ranunculus, have done their thing it is the turn of the annuals, the sweet peas and the flowers used for drying, known as the everlastings.

The demand for cut flowers in a house the size of Heligan during the nineteenth century would have been huge, armful after armful. Ornamental foliage would have been important too, and there would also have been a considerable call for potted plants such as lilies, and bulbs of every description as well as large evergreen container plants. The Flower Garden provided much of this, and it is Helen's job to see that it does so again, with the difference that many of the flowers will remain unpicked in their rows for the enjoyment of the visiting public.

The Vinery houses a collection of potted flowering bulbs of the type which would definitely have appealed to the lady of the house, and been well within the scope of the head gardener to grow. They include different species of *Eucomis*, *Polianthes*, *Tigridia*, *Hymenocallis* and *Nerine*. These are grown and looked after by Sylvia in addition to tending the Vinery's crop of dessert grapes. A good collection of outdoor species of lily are in Helen's domain, and they are found in the north-western corner of the garden, next to the Citrus House.

Behind the back wall of the Citrus House and Vineries, and a few paces to the north of the Head Gardener's Office, is the most recent addition to Heligan's range of glasshouses. Named Pencalenick, after

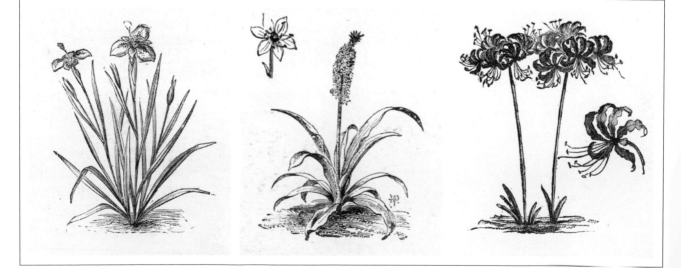

BEAUTIFUL *Hymenocallis* LINE THE PATH THROUGH THE VINERY TO THE CITRUS HOUSE, *opposite*. COSMOS IS ONE OF THE MOST POPULAR OF ALL ANNUAL GARDEN FLOWERS, *right*. IT CARRIES ON FLOWERING WELL INTO THE AUTUMN AND COMES IN ALL SHADES OF PINK AND RED AND ALSO WHITE. FLOWERS FOR CUTTING AND FOR THE BORDERS WERE VITAL TO THE VICTORIANS; THEY WERE THE PEAK OF HORTICULTURAL ACHIEVEMENT. *Below left, from left: Tigridia pavonia; Eucomis punctata; Nerine sarniensis.*

the estate near Truro from which it came, this single-span house holds a substantial collection of pelargoniums of the type that would once have graced many a table in Heligan House.

Bit by bit a picture can be built up of what was formerly grown, and where and why. Also in the Flower Garden under the north-east-facing wall are various shrubs that would have been used for their foliage: camellia, callistemon and even *Myrtus ugni* (now *Ugni molinae*), whose red berries have the distinct smell of strawberry Opal Fruits (now Starburst) and not a bad flavour too!

THE PEONY *Paeonia lactiflora* 'SARAH BERNHARDT' RESPLENDENT IN THE FLOWER GARDEN, *below.* ONLY FLOWERING FOR A SHORT PERIOD IN MAY, THEY ARE SO DELICATE THAT THE FEW WEEKS ARE WELL WORTH THE WAIT. A BIG BLOCK OF *Coreopsis* 'MAYFIELD GIANT', *opposite,* BRIGHTENS UP THE FLOWER GARDEN BENEATH THE VINERIES. *Previous pages,* THE GARDEN IN FULL BLOOM.

While biennials and bulbs are fitted in here and there, the main area for cut flowers, both annual and perennial, is the western side of the Flower Garden, beyond the dipping pool from which they were once watered. The sheer mass of these long rows of vivid flowers in mid-summer is not just a marvel, but unusual too. Compared to the flowers in the herbaceous borders, even the annuals grown in the Vegetable Garden, such as asters and antirrhinums, wonderful and eye-catching as they are, would struggle to match these borders' prodigious blocks of colour in every imaginable shade, where the demure blues of Miss Jekyll's *Nigella* mix with stripy-lollipop *Godetia* and girlie-pink *Clarkia*. It is a visual riot, and to see them all flowering at the same time is pure pleasure. Unlikely though it may seem, this is also what would have happened in Victorian times.

SEED SOWING

It is a tribute to the propagation skills of everyone concerned, in particular Kathy, Helen and Sylvia, that they can produce as many plants as they do, vegetable, flower and herb, from seed. The full life cycle of the plants is their responsibility, from seed sowing to harvest; the formidable level of skill and dedication needed in facing this challenge, and carrying it through to success, deserves to be understood by all who visit the gardens.

The first major responsibility is when, at the start of the season, Helen is faced with a mound of seed packets and has to begin the round of sowing. First off the rack are the sweet peas. Good germinators as a rule, they are relatively easy to establish. Things get a little trickier with the hardy annuals which may respond less well to the cool temperatures and poor light levels of springtime.

Growing from seed is a bit like flying, with the most danger at and soon after takeoff. The seed is sown, germinates and is then pricked out into modules. It is at this crucial stage, with the whole project still near its beginning, that there is the highest likelihood of something going wrong, in particular an attack from the damping-off fungus. Assuming that no signs of disease appear, the little plants can grow on

before being hardened off and planted out; but there can be worrying moments nonetheless.

After many years of tried and tested routines year on year, Heligan's gardeners are rarely surprised by new threats to their charges. They are only too aware of the menace posed by old acquaintances such as the wood pigeon and the carrot fly; but it is unlikely that anything new will come along without some prior warning to strike fear in their hearts. The New Zealand flatworm was anticipated some years ago, but never actually appeared in the garden. There has also been an attack on the rhododendrons by Sudden Oak Death; however, since this is one of the phytophthora group of fungal diseases, related to potato blight, it has been unlikely to damage annual vegetables or cut flowers.

PROPAGATION

In 2003 the need for plants with which to restock the gardens, and the huge turnover of sales in the busy Heligan Shop, led to the construction of a state-of-the-art propagation unit. It comprises two large glass-houses, two poly tunnels, cold frames, standing-out areas and a potting shed. In effect its foreman, Steve Phillips, now has charge of his own nursery.

Throughout Heligan's new beginnings, heritage plants from the gardens had always been propagated here. The idea of a purpose-built propagation unit came to fruition when Carolyn Webb, who now deals with plant sales, ran out of room. The new unit stands well away from the hubbub, next to the kennels behind the Bird Hide and below the composting areas. This allows Steve to get on with his important job unhindered. It is also a place where gardeners can come and ask him to look after something special or try and increase its stock. Here too, Steve has the time and space to break the dormancy of seeds that need periods of cold followed by warm treatment; and it is here that plants which are being tried out for the first time in the gardens, particularly in the Jungle, start their Heligan career.

The art of saving seed, of knowing when to sow it for the best possible chance of germination or whether to store it for a time, of taking cuttings

THE FOSTER & PEARSON COLD FRAME STANDS WIDE OPEN IN THE RESERVE GARDEN; AND SOME SPRING GREENS HAVE FOUND THEIR WAY INTO A COLD FRAME TO ESCAPE THE WINTER WEATHER AND ARE COMING TO FRUITION, *opposite*. STEVE PHILLIPS CATCHES UP ON SOME INDOOR WORK, *below*.

or reproducing plants by any means is a demanding job and Steve, who trained in horticulture at Merrist Wood and Rodbaston College near his native Birmingham, has all the skills required. One of his main allies is a mist-propagation unit with heated cables underneath. The combination of damp and warmth is the main asset of the modern-day propagator, since it enables most varieties to root quickly. Steve shades his glasshouses by spraying on a limewash known as summer cloud, which works to keep off the harmful rays of the sun.

It is here, in Steve's immaculate nursery, that duplicates are found of all the garden's favourites which are consistently requested in the shop. There are plants grown from seed, such as *Cornus capitata* and the handkerchief tree, *Davidia involucrata,* that grows in the Sundial Garden; and there are others that arrive in clumps from Helen in the Flower Garden. Perennials such as *Doronicum* and *Rudbeckia* have to be split, tidied up and repotted to make plants ready for sale. Those for whom Steve produces his plants have the assurance of a job well done, from which a usable or saleable plant is sure to result.

At the time of writing he is immensely pleased at having germinated the tamarind tree for Sylvia. Though ready for any undertaking, he is quick to recall his nervousness on his first day at work, and recounts his apprehension at the thought of taking some cuttings from one of Heligan's most highly valued plants, *Fuchsia robertiana,* allegedly named after one of the former head gardeners. When he arrived at the site of the plant, which climbs rampantly against the

THE MELON YARD, *left,* IS ALL CLEAN LINES ON A BRIGHT WINTER'S DAY LOOKING FROM THE FORCING FRAME ACROSS THE PINEAPPLE PIT TO THE MELON HOUSE AND THE ARCH INTO THE VEGETABLE GARDEN. THE FLOWER GARDEN, *right,* IS GETTING ITS SPRING CLOTHES ON. THE RHODODENDRONS HANGING OVER THE WALLS ARE A REMINDER OF HOW MUCH THE GARDEN HAD BECOME OUT OF CONTROL BEFORE THE RESTORATION BEGAN IN 1991.

THE GIANT BURMESE HONEY-SUCKLE *Lonicera hildebrandiana* RESIDES OVER THE ARCH THAT LEADS FROM THE MELON YARD INTO THE VEGETABLE GARDEN, *above*. VERY STRONGLY SCENTED, THE PLANT IS SURPRISINGLY HARDY AND SEEMS TO THRIVE IN THE HOT CONFINES OF THE ENCLOSED WALLED GARDEN.

outer south-facing wall of the Melon Yard, he discovered Jeremy Pederson giving it a heavy prune. All Steve's fears of attacking such an 'A'-list plant vanished, and he was given access to all the cuttings he could possibly use, without any responsibility for making any of the cuts himself.

Of the glasshouse, one is given over to propagating the collection of Victorian pelargoniums which, under the care of Mary Crowle, are raised in the greenhouse known as Pencalenick. Among these, Apple Blossom, Paton's Unique and Mr Henry Cox are three especially popular varieties. It was Philip who began this collection many years ago when he brought to the garden a very pretty red-flowered but un-named scented pelargonium. His purpose was to increase its stock, as pot plants for areas of the garden where flowers growing in containers are stood out to add some colour. It is typical of Heligan's potential for diversity that what started as a 'whimsy' — a favourite word amongst the staff — should become a serious horticultural venture.

THE
WIDER
GARDENS

1 THE PLEASURE GROUNDS

Heligan begins in the mind's eye. The romantic connotations of a 'lost' garden are strong. Clever marketing or not, the gardens at Heligan were indeed lost, to the undergrowth and overgrowth and to general decay. If a potential visitor knew only that this garden had undergone a major restoration and that previously it had been virtually abandoned, it might conjure up all manner of imaginative speculation. For many of those who are visiting Heligan for the first time there is a perception of mystery about the place. There has to be: simply the use of the word 'lost' in the title makes that clear. 'Lost? Lost to what? Lost where? Who lost the gardens? Did they fall off the map? Anyway, they are found now so let's go and visit them, they could be good.'

THE MUD MAID LIES WITH HER BACK TO THE SUN IN THE WEST, *opposite*. SITED IN THE WESTERN SHELTERBELT ON THE ROUTE TO THE JUNGLE, SHE IS THE GUARDIAN OF THE MOST IMPORTANT PART OF THE GARDEN. THE SHELTERBELT PROTECTS THE WHOLE OF HELIGAN FROM THE RAVAGES OF THE PREVAILING WESTERLY WINDS THAT CAN ROAR IN FROM THE ATLANTIC ONLY THIRTY ODD KILOMETRES AWAY. ALL IS CALM IN THE BOTTOM OF NEW ZEALAND, *above*.

As it happens they are quite easy to find, being about seven kilometres from the town of St Austell; also their reputation now goes before them. But when Tim Smit and John Nelson decided to restore them it was their absolute belief that the gardens should capture the imagination of everybody who came to see them, both during their work and long after the two men had finished. They were besotted with the place and everything in it, and for thousands upon thousands of people Heligan also holds a special place in their consciousness, as a place of mystery and magic and great beauty.

Whatever part of the garden any individual holds dearest, whether it is the Bee-Boles, the Pineapple Pit or the top pond in the Jungle, it was the intention of the project's founders that everyone should feel the magic of Heligan the moment they crossed the threshold and entered into the gardens. The place does hold magic within it, but that magic can only be sustained within the boundaries of the garden by those who tend its plants and nurture its spirit. Heligan's gardeners are its most important asset.

After crossing the drive to Heligan House suddenly you are into the gardens; and you are also entering the territory of the delightful Mary Crowle, who is in charge, apart from the productive gardens, of all the Pleasure Grounds.

This responsibility has fallen to Mary after some twelve years of gardening at Heligan; and no one is more in tune with the needs and requirements of the top half of the garden. So much of the limelight for

so many years has been directed at the Vegetable Garden and the Pineapple Pit or the great trees of the Jungle, whereas the workers in the Pleasure Grounds have somehow gone about their business without fanfare. It is the little things, the touches, that are noticeable about Mary's style of gardening.

Behind the *Magnolia campbellii* on Dovecote Lawn, on the far north boundary of the garden, is a semicircular bed containing a number of rhododendrons. Underneath them is a massive carpet of forget-me-nots and in front of the beds some handsome white benches. 'They go well with the white benches' is all Mary will say on the subject, but right away I can visualize the sea of tiny blue flowers blazing against the white garden furniture, along with the bare bones of the huge asiatic magnolia which in early spring is covered in large flowers of smoky pink, at exactly the same time that the forget-me-nots are at their best.

FIRST THINGS FIRST

Here too, as for most of the gardeners, the day begins with raking and clearing up. It is not just autumn leaves — the dastardly evergreen ilex oaks drop their foliage all year round, so that this needs to be raked up daily. The scuffmarks of the visitors' footprints need to be extinguished and the garden must be gently woken and smartened up for the day. For Mary, who has always been earlier to work than any of the other staff, often before seven in the morning, this means starting by the entrance and working inwards.

The Northern Gardens are horseshoe shaped, with the productive gardens filling the bottom half of the shoe. All around, the outsides belong to Mary and her helpers Trish Hogg, Jayne Delacoe (Mary's sister) and Carol Sherwood. All the paths have to be raked except on very wet days when raking makes more mess than a good impression.

Two other vital sharers in the upkeep of the Northern Gardens are James Hyland and Sam Corfield, who are to Mary what Mike Rundle and Clive Mildenhall are to Sylvia Travers in the productive gardens – an unfailing source of muscle, and increasingly skilled backup. They are responsible for mowing all the lawns, which comprise Flora's

M*agnolia* × *soulangeana* 'LENNEI' IS AN ORIGINAL PLANT FOUND IN THE GARDEN KNOWN AS NEW ZEALAND, *left.* THIS VENERABLE OLD FLOWERING TREE LIES GENTLY ON ITS SIDE, GIVING UP ITS BEAUTIFUL PINK FLOWERS YEAR ON YEAR.

Sudden oak death has led to some drastic intervention throughout the estate but nowhere more than on Heligan's magical Cornish red rhododendrons, *opposite*. The raising of the famous plant's skirts off the soil is perhaps the most dramatic move. Mary and Trish prune off any infected shoots and leaves, *below*.

Green and the grass in the Sundial Garden as well as the Bee-Boles lawn and other odd bits and pieces. They also have the hedges to clip throughout the Northern Gardens. This means shaping the upside-down *Griselinia* arch at the Northern Summerhouse lookout point, along with all the box hedges in the Vegetable Garden and the Flower Garden: a considerable and a very important framework to keep looking good. They are tireless workers, these two, and whilst still junior members of staff they are the future of Heligan.

Although not part of the morning rake-around, other plants drop leaves that have to be picked up on a weekly basis. These are the Cornish Red rhododendrons whose once great mound-like forms dominated the skirts of Flora's Green, the large expanse of lawn at the very top of the garden and the first big space that becomes visible on entry into the gardens. Flora's Green and its surrounds are the highlight of the Pleasure Grounds and the lawn is like a source pool for the rest of the garden in that all directions feed off from it.

One recent change is that the domed rhododendrons which once swept the edges of the lawn have become mushroom-shaped, their skirts raised so that no contact may be had between leaf and soil. Sudden Oak Death has changed the face of Heligan, and resulted in the removal of a lot of plant matter in the process. In fairness much of the *Rhododendron ponticum* that has been affected would have been removed in time anyway; the onset of fungal disease has merely hastened its removal and incidentally opened up new areas for planting. This is a good thing – like all great gardens Heligan has been consistently changing since it was at its height in Victorian times and it will continue to change so long as the will and the vision are there.

Sudden Oak Death (SOD) brought much extra work to Mary and her helpers. On the instructions of the Ministry responsible, DEFRA, the crowns of the old Cornish Reds had to be raised, by reducing the skirts at their base to roughly 1.2 metres above ground level. Heligan's Managing Director, Peter Stafford, was among those who heard the call to arms over this crisis, and rallied to the cause by lending a hand with the pruning loppers. It must have been heart-rending to make radical pruning

cuts to such totemic and time-honoured plants as the Cornish Reds. Throughout Cornwall their graceful shape has long been a defining feature in the gardens of many great houses.

As a result of cutting back these plants they do indeed look healthy. What does concern Mary, thinking like a true gardener, is that they might be a little top heavy, for to be bare legged as they now are is not their natural way of growing.

From Flora's Green there are two 'rides', Eastern and Western, which run in a north–south direction down each side of the garden, with the productive gardens, the Ravine and the area known as New Zealand between them. Halfway down the Eastern Ride a large block of *R. ponticum* was removed on account of SOD. Lying opposite, and on its side as it has done for as long as anyone can remember and certainly since the start of the restoration, is a very fine specimen of *Magnolia x soulangeana* 'Lennei'. In the course of trying to keep this shrub free of weeds Mary came across a number of shoots from it that had layered, or rooted, themselves. She dug them up, and replanted two of them in the gap left by the removal of the *R. ponticum*: a good example of a potential problem successfully resolved. Stricken as it is, the old magnolia will not live forever; but now its memory will be prolonged in the shape of its newly planted offspring.

HELIGAN IS HOME TO MANY RHODODENDRONS WHICH HAVE HYBRIDIZED NATURALLY AND AS SUCH REMAIN UNNAMED, *opposite* AND *below*. MANY ARE THE OFFSPRING FROM THE PLANT HUNTING EXPLOITS OF SIR JOSEPH HOOKER, WHO BROUGHT MANY SPECIMENS OF *R. arboreum* TO HELIGAN IN THE 1850S.

DECORATIVE GARDENING

The two Rides are rather vaguely delineated, in that they are dominated by a canopy of large trees such as beech and oak whilst the shrub layer largely consists of rhododendron, hydrangea, and camellia. Having an eye to the great need for year-round colour, Mary is forever identifying more intimate corners into which she can plant further quantities of cyclamen. Mostly she introduces spring flowering varieties, as the autumn flowerers would have to compete with colour from the foliage of other plants and would therefore make less of an impact.

One of Mary's concerns has always been planting and the use of containers in general. As well as having an eye for good design, she is also a wizard

Hydrangeas, *above,* usually divide people into opposing camps of love or loathe. But whatever anybody says about them, they are very much 'of the country' and are found throughout the gardens and the county. Cyclamen, *left,* are perennial favourites.

*C*amellia japonica 'LADY CLARE', *right*, IS ONE OF THE FIRST VARIETIES TO COME OUT IN THE LATE WINTER. ONE OF A NUMBER OF UNNAMED CAMELLIAS THAT FOUND THEIR WAY INTO THE GARDENS IN THE NINETEENTH CENTURY, *below*.

THE ITALIAN GARDEN, *above* AND *opposite,* WAS COMPLETELY REBUILT BY JOHN NELSON AT THE START OF THE RESTORATION AND IS NOW ONE OF THE MOST POPULAR AND INTIMATE SPACES AT HELIGAN. THE LOOKS ON THE FACES OF VISITORS WHEN THEY FIND THIS LITTLE OASIS OF CALM IS OFTEN ONE OF SHEER DELIGHT.

propagator. In the Northern Summerhouse garden, she has a challenging palette with which to play. This area is tucked away in the northeast corner of the gardens, from where there is a fabulous view eastwards over St Austell Bay and up the English Channel on a clear day. The possibilities offered by such a site were reduced some years ago when the entire garden was paved with slate. The intimacy of the place was removed at a stroke, to be replaced by a harsh grey gloom. The small but pretty rectangular pond that sits amidst all this greyness has as its main flowering plant a finely formed white water lily. To pick up the effect of these lilies, and take the eye from the overpowering slate slabs, Mary has placed square terracotta pots at the four corners of the pool. Each contains two varieties of *Thalictrum aquilegiifolium*, a delicate-leaved perennial with baby purple ball-shaped flowers; and a seedling of *Plagianthus betulinus*. The two kinds of plant stand just less than a metre in height and have similar foliage, that of *P. betulinus* being slightly more crinkly than the leaves of the *Thalictrum*. Both varieties are upright, one a herbaceous perennial, the other a tree seedling without a flower. The mixture is a stroke of genius, being unassuming yet sophisticated, in a way that takes the onlooker's attention away from the harshness of the paving and draws it right back to the pool.

The Italian Garden was completely restored in 1991, and since that time it has matured into itself. Here Mary and Trish have skilfully been nurturing a fine collection of plants. Heligan lies in a corridor of uncertainty where frost-tender plants are concerned, and the Italian

Garden is packed with specimens which are right on the border of survival. *Isoplexis canariensis* is a typical example. This native of the Canary Islands and Madeira usually needs to be wrapped up in hessian sacking over the winter but after watching it over the years Mary and Trish have decided that there is no further need for such an extravagant degree of protection. In the meantime they have toughened it up, allowing a big *Actinidia chinensis* and a hibiscus to protect it. Similarly, in the case of the garden's *Echiums*, it was felt that only so much protection could be given; and even though the winter of 2004/2005 produced the longest spell of sub-zero temperatures for many years, the delicate plants in the Italian Garden survived. It takes a steady judgement to work on the edge like this. The risks are high, not least in a garden like Heligan, whose *Geranium maderense*, for example, is not fond of frost, nor is the delicious Chilean jasmine, *Mandevilla laxa*, which clambers over the roof of the summerhouse.

NEW BEGINNINGS

The most memorable task undertaken by Mary and her team is perhaps the northerly extension of the New Zealand garden, which runs between the Eastern Ride and the Vegetable Garden. The original garden was planted by the Tremaynes, who throughout the nineteenth century and earlier were interested in all new-found plant varieties

TREE FERNS, *left*, HAVE BECOME A SIGNATURE PLANT OF HELIGAN — EVEN DOWN TO BECOMING PART OF THE LOGO OF THE GARDENS. THEY ARE PLENTIFUL IN BOTH THE NORTHERN GARDENS AND THE JUNGLE AND ENCAPSULATE THE SPIRIT OF THE PLACE MORE THAN ANY OTHER PLANT. A MUCH MORE RECENT ARRIVAL IS THE CHATHAM ISLAND FORGET-ME-NOT, *above,* WHICH IS ANOTHER QUITE MAGNIFICENT PLANT.

that might grow at Heligan. With the arrival in the 1880s of the tree fern, *Dicksonia antarctica*, from south-eastern Australia, courtesy of Treseder's Nursery, it quickly became clear that many antipodean plants were suited to the warm, damp climate offered by much of Cornwall. Heligan was no exception, and the New Zealand garden is filled with much-admired plants from that part of the world. In 2003 it was decided to expand this area up the side of the Vegetable Garden to where it meets the Northern Summerhouse. Fittingly the new garden ends close to the point where a fine specimen of *Podocarpus totara*, the New Zealand yew, was very much intact at the start of the restoration. The first major plantings were three *Magnolia grandiflora* 'Gallisoniensis', which go well with the *M. delavayi*, another splendid plant which was already in the prime of its life.

Here, too, Mary can cultivate the Chatham Island forget-me-not (*Myosotidium hortensia*) for fun, where once it was considered a difficult plant to raise. She also has the care of such delights as *Tecomanthe*

Trish hogg at work in the yard where she and mary crowle work to produce so many plants in pots for the garden, *below.* although there is no house for which to grow plants, there are tea rooms, tables, offices and nooks and crannies all over heligan where a bowl of bulbs or a scented pelargonium can work wonders. all is provided by mary and trish. *Opposite,* the flower stem of *Agapanthus orientalis* after shedding its petals.

speciosa, an evergreen frost-tender climber found in the woodland of tropical New Zealand; from the same country there are species of the deciduous shrub *Carmichaelia*. *Senecio compactus* (*Brachyglottis compacta*) grows here too, a handsome mound-shaped shrub that produces frothy yellow flower heads in summer; also the feather duster palm, *Rhopalostylis sapida*, from New Zealand and Chatham Island. The Victorians had to take pains in learning how to grow their new acquisitions; so too must Mary in tending any fresh arrivals. To help with this she has engaged the services of Carol Sherwood who divides her time between the New Zealand garden and assisting Helen in the Flower Garden.

OLD FRIENDS

The Sundial Garden is also Mary's domain. Ever since the first brambles were cleared, she has been closely involved and took part in the initial plantings in the spring of 1995. It has been here, out of the gaze of the public eye, that she has really learned her horticulture.

Some plants in this garden's hundred-feet-long borders are not easy to grow: for example *Romneya coulteri*, with its subtle grey foliage and tantalizing white flower dashed with red, can be persuaded to flower well and consistently, even though it would really prefer drier conditions. The variegated kiwi, *Actinidia kolomikta*, which climbs the wall between the *Stauntonia* and a beautifully flowering *Rosa* 'Russeliana', is not easy either. Although it is extremely vigorous and reaches the top of the wall, it still prompted one visitor to raise a few smiles by enquiring whether it would grow in this country.

The south-facing border of the Sundial Garden, beneath an ancient handkerchief tree which casts its shade over the east end of the garden, was described in the *Gardeners' Chronicle* of 1896 as the finest herbaceous border in the country. With this in mind, it is still being worked to the 1995 planting plan done by Toby Musgrave and Chris Gardner, consisting entirely of period-correct plants, and which few would deny similar status today.

Another responsibility for Mary and her team is

THE SUNDIAL GARDEN IS THE VERY SOUTHERN MOST OF THE WALLED GARDENS AT HELIGAN, *opposite*. IT LIES DIRECTLY BENEATH THE FLOWER GARDEN AND IS MADE UP OF TWO HERBACEOUS BORDERS RUNNING EITHER SIDE OF THE LAWN WHICH HOLDS THE SUNDIAL IN THE MIDDLE. THE ENTIRE GARDEN IS OVERLOOKED BY A VERY OLD SPECIMEN OF THE HANDKERCHIEF TREE, *Davidia involucrata. Below, Aquilegia vulgaris* 'FLORE PLENO'. *Bottom, Corydalis flexuosa.*

the production of huge amounts of plants in pots for the garden. There are many areas that demand year-round colour. They include the Covered Area, which includes the entrance to the Tea Room, with some rather eccentric 'hay racks' hanging from the wall opposite the offices; also the area around the shop. and the walk down to the ticket office. All these are a mass of colour and constantly changing. There is the pavilion in the Italian Garden, and the Northern Summerhouse too, to be constantly planted out with colour. From late summer Mary, Trish, Jane and Carol must get to work on the huge deliveries of bulbs that begin to appear.

Bulbs are not the only plants that are raised to flower in pots; you could find all sorts of things in Mary's glasshouses which she has propagated from a slip or a cutting that has come her way. There are *Aeoniums*; also an amazing collection of *Hoya carnosa* dotted around the place, sweet juice oozing from their stems; and fuchsias and erigeron. Anything will find its way into a pot and onto a ledge if it appeals to Mary's good taste as being appropriate and pretty, and apt to brighten up the garden.

From early beginnings digging over the infant Flower Garden to planting up the Sundial Garden and overseeing the many changes to the Northern Summerhouse, over the years Mary has had a hand in almost everything that has happened in the garden at Heligan. One special charge of hers has always been the huge stand of *Gunnera manicata* that grows beneath the Wishing Well, in the bottom south-east corner of the Northern Gardens.

These plants were planted on a bund, a raised bed of soil, where overspill collects from the well. They began as small plants, looking vulnerable, even out of place. Every year in spring Mary would give them a feed of well-rotted manure. She would mound up the nutrient-rich organic matter around the base of the stems and watch her charges flourish and grow. At the end of the season, when the huge leaves began to turn brown, crack and die, she would cut them off at the bottom of the stems and cart the tattered ones off to the compost heap. The good ones she would place over the crowns until they too

cracked and broke down. She would then take a long roll of hessian sacking and wrap the crowns up in it to protect them from the frost, having first given them another good mulching of well-rotted manure. Every spring, after any threat of heavy frost has passed, Mary unwraps the gunnera and lets them breathe in the soft spring air and see the light of day. Throughout the summer she waters the plants whenever there is anything approaching what might be called a dry spell. Now the gunnera have reached triffid-like heights, and all through being cared for with love and devotion.

On a summer's morning it is one of the greatest of pleasures to find yourself in that little corner of the Northern Gardens. Charles Fleming will be raking up leaves and tidying the paths and Mary will be watering the gunnera: two of Heligan's stalwarts going about their business, as always solidly professional.

Verbena bonariensis, *left,* IS ONE
OF THE MOST PROLIFIC SELF-
SEEDERS OF ANY HERBACEOUS PLANT.
HERE IT HAS OVERTAKEN THE SOUTH-
ERN BORDER IN THE SUNDIAL GARDEN
WITH DRAMATIC EFFECT, THE WHOLE
SWATHE PUNCTURED ONLY BY THE
BENCH AND THE CLUMP OF WHITE
AGAPANTHUS.

2 THE JUNGLE

The Jungle is the given name for the valley garden that runs from below Heligan House almost to the small fishing port of Mevagissey. There are barely a few fields between the very bottom of the Jungle and the sea, but they are mostly unnoticed except by anyone wanting access to the coast. In Victorian times and before, the motives of such people were plentiful, and often murky.

THE PROXIMITY OF HELIGAN TO THE SEA IS EVIDENT FROM VARIOUS VANTAGE POINTS IN THE GARDEN NOTABLY THE NORTHERN SUMMERHOUSE. THIS PHOTOGRAPH, *above*, IS TAKEN FROM TREGISKEY CROSS HALFWAY BETWEEN HELIGAN, PENTEWAN AND MEVAGISSEY AND IS TYPICAL OF THE TYPE OF VALLEY THAT MIGHT BE ATTACHED TO A GARDEN SUCH AS HELIGAN AND HOLD A PLANT SUCH AS, *opposite*, *Phoenix canariensis*.

Cornwall is attractive to many people, for a variety of reasons; but for most the biggest draw, apart from its beaches, has been and always will be its coastline. From Kingsand Bay, close to Saltash on its English Channel coast, looking westwards right around the Land's End peninsula to Bude on the Atlantic Ocean coast and the second, northern, border with Devon, the coastline is indented by creeks, coves, estuaries and caves which evoke some of the mystery, excitement or dread that are evident in some of the histories of Cornwall. There is still a touch of credibility about the tales of smugglers, wreckers and plotters depicted by Daphne du Maurier in such classics as *Jamaica Inn* and *Frenchman's Creek*. Smuggling is no modern invention, and probably secret tunnels did exist. In many cases, too, it was the local landowners who, if not complicit, nonetheless turned a blind eye to what went on. Often it was they, after all, who owned the land over which the contraband had to pass on the way to its final destination.

ITS GEOGRAPHY

The tithe map of 1839 shows the Jungle as an orchard and a pond, sitting just below Heligan House. A strange choice of site: as the orchard for a house the size of Heligan, it was unusually small. It was also oddly sited on any terms. Frost drains downhill; there is a considerable drop from the house to the pond; and apples are quite unsuited to growing in or at least just above a frost pocket. The map offers a partial explanation, in that it shows no evidence of any sizeable orchard anywhere within the boundaries of the Northern Gardens. Also it may have been possible that the cultivation of apples for dessert, cooking and the making of cider was farmed out to a tenant of the Tremayne family.

The Jungle is a steep-sided valley through which there runs a series of four ponds fed by the overspill of water from the Northern Gardens and various underground springs. The first impression on any gardener makes them wonder how it is possible to work such terrain; the second makes them ask: how on earth did they manage in 1860? The answer to the latter question is: very well — but only because nineteenth-century gardeners used of necessity to make the modern equivalent look a bit weak. Gardening on a hillside can be a strain on the body, since heaving anything uphill is a sweat. No machinery can get into the Jungle, so that as in the Vegetable Garden, everything has to done by hand. Any necessary materials can be brought right up to most of the Jungle's top end by machine; but inside the garden everything is only moveable by hand.

THE JUNGLE IS DOMINATED BY ITS THUNDEROUS COLLECTION OF *Rhododendron arboreum*, *right*, COURTESY OF SIR JOSEPH HOOKER. THEY CLIMB UP THE SIDES OF THE VALLEY WALLS AND REACH INCREDIBLE HEIGHTS PROVIDING THE SHELTER FOR THE MORE TENDER PLANTS ON THE VALLEY FLOOR SUCH AS THE TREE FERNS.

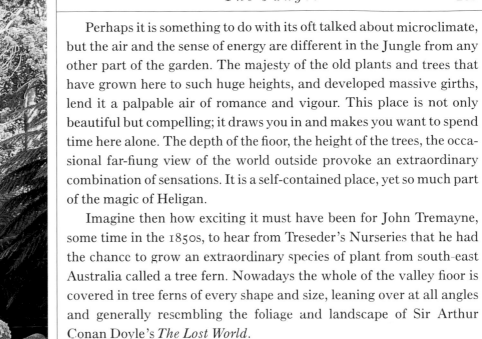

Perhaps it is something to do with its oft talked about microclimate, but the air and the sense of energy are different in the Jungle from any other part of the garden. The majesty of the old plants and trees that have grown here to such huge heights, and developed massive girths, lend it a palpable air of romance and vigour. This place is not only beautiful but compelling; it draws you in and makes you want to spend time here alone. The depth of the fioor, the height of the trees, the occasional far-fiung view of the world outside provoke an extraordinary combination of sensations. It is a self-contained place, yet so much part of the magic of Heligan.

Imagine then how exciting it must have been for John Tremayne, some time in the 1850s, to hear from Treseder's Nurseries that he had the chancc to grow an extraordinary species of plant from south-east Australia called a tree fern. Nowadays the whole of the valley fioor is covered in tree ferns of every shape and size, leaning over at all angles and generally rescmbling the foliage and landscape of Sir Arthur Conan Doyle's *The Lost World*.

RESTORATION

The foreman in charge of the Jungle is Mike Friend, who is assisted by Cindy Clench and a handful of students and irregular volunteers. It represents an awesome task for this devoted band, but they have done great things and at their present rate of achievement they are destined for yet more.

DOWN IN THE DEPTHS OF THE JUNGLE, *left,* WHERE GARDENING BECOMES AN EXERCISE IN SURVIVAL, ESPECIALLY IN WINTER. SUMMER CAN BE DIFFICULT ENOUGH TOO AND NO ONE WOULD WANT TO TANGLE WITH THE SPINY STEMS AND FOLIAGE OF *Gunnera manicata,* NEAR LEFT FOREGROUND — EXCEPT PERHAPS THE FOREMAN, MIKE FRIEND, *right,* WHO HAS DONE SO MUCH TO CARRY ON THE DEVELOPMENT OF THIS UNIQUE GARDEN.

THE VIEW FROM JUST BENEATH
THE HOUSE, *above.* THIS IS THE
FIRST OF FOUR PONDS THAT DESCEND
GENTLY THROUGH THE INTENSELY
FOLIATED AND STEEPLY SIDED
JUNGLE GARDEN.

It is worth returning, briefly, to the starting point of the restoration in the early 1990s when the Jungle was a complete mess. The four ponds were silted up and the valley sides and floor were choked with pernicious invaders such as Japanese knotweed, bramble, dock and every other imaginable gardening horror. Self-sown and quick-growing trees, sometimes unfairly called 'weed trees', such as sycamore and ash were everywhere and the first nineteenth-century plantings had either disappeared and died under the rampant growth or had shot up, looking for the light, and turned into outsize giants.

Today the emphasis continues on restoring the garden but also on improving it by bringing in new varieties, to take full advantage both of its extraordinary geographical location and aspect and of its history. The boundaries of experimentation are being pushed back once again. Plants such as Vireya rhododendrons and *Griselinia lucida* are being tried out as potentially suited to this garden that as recently as ten years ago would not have been chosen.

The top pond, the Jungle's source pool, is a mass of water lilies and hovering blue dragonflies. It is overlooked by a giant tree fern, and a display of *Rhododendron arboreum* hangs at improbable angles over the pond, each spring dropping its red blossoms into the water. This memorable sight is a fabulous introduction to the wilds and glories of the Jungle. From this vantage point the view down the densely planted treescape is strange and almost daunting: you can see down the valley for a long way, but everything that you can see might as well be part of a south-east Asian rainforest.

The most exciting recent development in the Jungle has been the building and planting of what is now semi-officially known as the protea bed. This got its name because of what may turn out to be its star among plants, *Protea cynaroides*, the King Protea. Proteas are natives of South Africa and the only other place in the British Isles where they grow in profusion is in the Abbey Gardens on Tresco, in the Isles of Scilly. Though not totally frost-proof, neither are they completely vulnerable. Given a good start and a little luck, they could become the centrepiece of this spectacular new planting.

Formerly this part of the Jungle was a mix of smaller beds, before being turned into one huge bed held together by an 'infinity' stone wall, the work of the estate's maintenance team, comprising Adrian Burrows, Lee Watkins and Dave Bulbeck. As you approach the Jungle from East Lawn, you pass through a young shelterbelt of mixed native species and an older one of *Pinus radiata*, the Monterey pine, an important shelter tree throughout the maritime areas of Cornwall. At this point the view down the valley is blocked out by a very old *Cryptomeria japonica* which is the first tree in the line of sight. Next to it is a sycamore which may be even older and around which is the new bed. The wall, however, is invisible. Because of the way the land falls away and how the wall has been built, all you can see are the plants in the

FURTHER ON DOWN IS LOST VALLEY. THIS BLOCK OF ANCIENT WOODLAND IS BEING TAMED AND WEED TREES SUCH AS SYCAMORE REMOVED TO ALLOW LIGHT TO PENETRATE. TONY TRINGHAM STANDS GUARD OVER THE CHARCOAL BURNER AS THE WISPS OF SMOKE TRICKLE OUT OF THE CHIMNEY, *below.*

bed and those below. It is cleverly done; but then the Jungle is about plants, not hard landscaping. The eye is next drawn to the new planting, and over the top of that to the rhododendrons which lean above the top pond, itself almost entirely obscured by a thick clump of bamboo. Steps lead down from the new bed to the pond, where a gap has been cut in the bamboo and a platform built enabling visitors to see over and into the pond.

Among the many plants being tried for the first time in the new bed is the South African *Restios* and, from the same country, *Thamnochortus insignis*, a dark green and brown, tufted grass-like plant that grows to a thick and impressive 1.5 to 2 metres in height. *Telopea speciosissima*, known down under as the Sydney waratah, is a handsome Australian shrub with brilliant red flowers, and one that the Jungle team hope will also prove hardy enough for the climate of Cornwall.

Mike Friend, a member of the Heligan staff since 1997, has a terrific feel for what will and what won't flourish in any particular location. He was closely involved in developing the New Zealand garden in the Northern Gardens in the late 1990s and is a knowledgeable and sensitive plantsman. Other new varieties include *Lampranthus*, formerly known as mesembryanthemums, or even 'mezzies', and under his watchful eye these have every chance of succeeding.

Mike's enthusiasms also number among them the *Leucadendrons*, not least *L.* 'Safari Sunset' and *L.* 'Fireglow'. These South African natives are in the same family as the proteas, which they resemble in their small upright foliage and cone-like flowers. The same area features *Protea* 'Pink Ice', a form of the King Protea. When this bed reaches maturity, with these South African and Australasian plants in full riotous bloom against the backdrop of their Asian relatives the magnolias and rhododendrons, it will provide the Jungle with an extraordinary entrance.

The framework of the Jungle is provided by some exceptional surviving trees. One of the Tremaynes had an enthusiasm for conifers, with the result that some fine examples of these are still left. Like them or not, Monkey Puzzles, *Araucaria araucana*, from Chile, make swaggering trees and have a prehistoric look about them that makes them perfect for the Jungle. The New Zealand yew, *Podocarpus totara*, is another evergreen conifer which has grown to a great height, and which stands sentinel between the second and third ponds. *Trachycarpus fortunei*, the chusan palm, and the tree ferns are everywhere and throughout the valley there are pockets of *Crinodendron hookerianum* and

Echium candicans, opposite, IS JUST ONE OF A HUGE COLLECTION OF PLANTS FROM ALL OVER THE WORLD THAT HAVE FOUND THEIR WAY INTO THE JUNGLE AND HAVE THRIVED. THE MICRO CLIMATE IS SUCH THAT VERY LITTLE FROST PENETRATES AND THE SALT FROM THE EASTERLY GALES BLOWS OVER THE TOP OF THE CANOPY. IT IS WARM AND DAMP AND PROVIDES EXCELLENT GROWING CONDITIONS FOR MANY PLANTS. *Below, Bambusa aurea.*

THE BOTTOM POND, *below*, WHERE A HUGE COLLECTION OF TREE FERNS MARKS THE END OF THE JUNGLE AND THE BEGINNING OF LOST VALLEY, HAS BEEN BRIDGED AND PLANTED UP WITH PLANTS FOR YEAR ROUND INTEREST. THE CHUSAN PALM, *Trachycarpus fortunei*, *opposite*, GROWS RAM-ROD STRAIGHT BENEATH THE CANOPY LAYER.

Rhododendron arboreum. The second and third ponds have great swathes of gunnera and the American skunk cabbage, *Lysichiton americanus*, a vivid yellow when in flower in early spring, both adding some shrubby and herbaceous elements to the Jungle.

At one stage the Jungle was known as the Japanese Garden, which may have been because bamboo is well represented here. Its introduction was perhaps the work of Jack, John Tremayne's son, who also built the Italian Garden. An ancient picture of the subsequent Jungle garden reveals a golden Buddha in the recesses of the summerhouse, possibly a relic of a visit to Japan.

The Jungle's most noticeable bamboo is *Chimonobambusa quadrangularis*, which forms a dense tunnel on the western side of the garden's boardwalk. Being very vigorous, it was once cut regularly to supply the Vegetable Garden with beanpoles. Though the tunnel remains thick and impenetrable, Mike has introduced several more varieties of bamboo, from Mike Bell's nursery at Wadebridge in north Cornwall. In a move away from simply growing the traditional thick stand of bamboo, on the advice of Bell the clumps have been thinned with the result that they appear to have been brought from the background to the foreground. Also, and this is particularly attractive, the light is now filtered through the plants, in the process picking out the different colours and shapes of their stems. The dead leaves form a soft brown carpet underfoot and there are areas around the Jungle's thickets of bamboo where one might expect to see a tiger walk around the corner.

Large changes have been made to improve the bottom pond. The wooden bridge across the pond now affords a proper look over the water and is a fitting end to a walk taking the visitor all the way to the bottom of the Jungle. A handsome Victorian style of planting has been followed here, with the use of herbaceous and bulbous plants on the pond edges as well as by the little stream that feeds down from the third pond. One wonderful plant is *Cardiocrinum giganteum*, the giant Himalayan lily; this reaches over two metres in height with huge white flowers from halfway up the stem. A native of Nepal, the *Cardiocrinum* is happiest in the shade and was

included in Victorian plantings when the Jungle was first springing to life. Also here are some extraordinary lobelias: *L.* 'Bee's Flame' has rich red flowers to go with its dark foliage, and there is *L. tupa*, also red and tall growing but with slightly lighter foliage. Bamboos flourish on top of the wall of the dam and all around are tree ferns and Chusan palms (*Trachycarpus fortunei*), each an example of the exotic foliage for which the Jungle has become famous. There are ligularias and primulas, and *Pontederia cordata* grows on the edge of the pond, where Adrian has cleverly built an underwater ledge for planting.

Between the Jungle's second and third ponds a new bed on the east side has been named 'Swords and Palms'. This bold piece of landscaping was probably inspired by the arrival many years ago of a solitary Phoenix palm. At first this plant resided in the Flower Garden, in a purpose-built wooden container on the edge of the brick terrace in front of the Vinery. Like a cuckoo in the nest it soon began to outgrow its home and the decision was taken to move it to the Jungle.

It is as well that most of the palms and succulents prefer a slightly acidic soil, since that is what they have in the Jungle. Here are found the spiky shapes and the succulents, the pointed and the flat, the big, the bold and the jungly plants. This is the home of *Echium pininana*, with its lance-shaped leaves, and huge flower spike covered in early summer with tiny blue blossoms, and *E. candicans*, the Pride of Madeira, a slightly shorter, multi-stemmed equivalent. There are agaves and yuccas and even a plant which, arriving in a batch of

A PATH ON THE EASTERN SIDE OF THE JUNGLE AND MORE ECHIUM, *left. Right,* TWO *Echium pininana* STAND TALL WITH A SPECIMEN OF *Cordyline australis*, INDICATING THE EXTRAORDINARY HEIGHTS TO WHICH THESE BIENNIALS GROW. IT IS A TRAGEDY TO THINK THAT THESE NATIVES OF THE CANARY ISLES DIE AT THE AGE OF TWO, HAVING FLOWERED FOR ONE SEASON ONLY.

yuccas, was mistaken for one — only to be recognized later as a bonus Furcraea. So far it seems very healthy and, if it matures, visitors will find it worth the entry money just to see a Furcraea in full flower. Though the plant is no more than a metre in height, it comprises a large rosette of lance-shaped leaves each about a metre in length. Come summer, a flower spike appears from the centre of the rosette and grows up and up until it reaches six metres and more, at which point it produces creamy bell-shaped flowers on the end of short branches. It seeds freely and, if the weather is not too cold, the germination rate can be high, yielding many more tiny Furcraeas to be lifted, potted and cultivated. It is most impressive and very unusual in the UK to see a Furcraea fully mature and in flower.

Puya chilensis flourishes here too. This plant has always grown well in the Sundial Garden, and is now expected to make its presence felt in the Jungle. Its leaves are savagely spiky, to the extent that, in the Flower Garden, Mary, like Trish with the yuccas in the Italian Garden, keeps its foliage under control to stop children scraping themselves. If you lose a tennis ball in a *Puya* there is no getting it back. It is a bromeliad and like the pineapples in the Pit it will produce a flower head almost the shape of a pineapple.

One critical component of the Jungle Garden is the Woodland team, comprising Jim Briggs, Matt Caley and Tony Tringham. They are the people to call on when tree surgery is needed. Agile when climbing trees and equally competent on the ground, they are employed to shape the gardens as required. They can be found anywhere in the gardens, taking down dangerous branches or carrying out essential pruning cuts to trees throughout the estate.

The Jungle is a bewitching garden and is emerging like a butterfly from its chrysalis after some very lean years. The amount of work this has taken has been enormous, but its ever widening collection of plants and the sheer enthusiasm with which it is now tended has guaranteed it a future and a very interesting one at that. As successors to those who first planted it in the nineteenth century it has attracted a team that will follow the garden's early traditions and once more make it a special part of the gardens at Heligan.

AND THEN THERE IS MAINTENANCE: THE SIMPLE ACT OF WEEDING IN THE JUNGLE, *above,* AND THE VERY COMPLEX, INVOLVED AND DANGEROUS ACT OF CLIMBING TREES TO CARRY OUT IMPORTANT SURGERY, *opposite.* ALL SKILLS ARE COVERED TO KEEP THE GARDENS UP TO SCRATCH.

3 CONCLUSION

Each morning in the gardens at Heligan there is a moment when everything seems to stand still. It is as though, all the gardeners having departed, the garden has an interlude, a breathing space, in which it can be alone with itself. The doors are open, the paths raked clear for numberless feet, and there descends an immense calm. It is usually now, before the visitors arrive and while the staff are headed for their crib, when almost always at this particular time of the mid-morning there comes a strong sense that Heligan responds absolutely to being gardened.

A N ABUNDANT SPECTACLE, *left,* THE HARVEST AT THE HEIGHT OF THE SEASON IN HELIGAN'S VEGETABLE GARDEN. *Following pages,* MIDSUMMER IN THE FLOWER GARDEN. THE FOREGROUND SHOWS THE ROWS OF VEGETABLE AND SALAD CROPS NEATLY INTERRUPTED BY THE BUSY WORK OF A MOLE.

From the chaos of the early 1990s, when the restoration was getting under way, order has arisen, almost as if the garden were being run by its original staff, except that now there is no rigorous pre-dawn starting time nor the horrific punishments, as I imagine there were, for latecomers. Everything works very well, so that everyone knows what to do and is allowed to get on with their tasks unhindered. This creates a tremendous sense of well being, even though the jobs that must be done can include some extraordinarily hard manual labour.

That the visitors keep coming is no surprise to me for two reasons. The first is that Heligan has and always will be well gardened. No garden which is open as a visitor attraction can sustain itself unless it maintains the highest possible standards. If it does not the public will not come — that is assured. It was a wise move to follow Victorian traditions for the restoration and continuation of the horticulture because it meant that little would be left to chance, and I feel that this shines through — nothing was half done in the nineteenth century either. There is a strong feeling of authenticity about Heligan; the results are there to see.

The second is the inherent magic that runs through the place. It has something, and people feel it. There is no point trying to describe it but there is something there, in the air, in the smells, in the soil and in the plants, just a little touch of wonder which is very compelling.

Heligan is a happy garden and one very much at peace with itself. This is entirely due to those who garden here, for they are people ready to come out in all weathers and who are not afraid to tackle any task. The well being of the garden is in their hearts because Heligan is more than a job: it is a way of life.

Sources

Isabella Beeton (1861) *Mrs. Beeton's The Book of Household Management Comprising information for the Mistress, Housekeeper, Cook, Kitchen-Maid, Butler, Footman, Coachman, Valet, Upper and Under House-Maids, Lady's-Maid, Maid-of-all-Work, Laundry-Maid, Nurse and Nurse-Maid, Monthly Wet and Sick Nurses, etc. etc. also Sanitary, Medical, & Legal Memoranda: with a History of the Origin, Properties, and Uses of all Things Connected with Home Life and Comfort.* (S.O. Beeton, London).

—— *Vegetables. How they should be Cooked and Served Up, &c.* (Ward, Lock and Tyler, London).

W.D. Drury (ed.) (1900), *The Book of Gardening: A Handbook of Horticulture* (L. Upcott Gill, London).

William Forsyth, (1824), *A Treatise on the Culture and Management of Fruit Trees; in which a New Method of Pruning and Training is Fully Described* (Longman, London).

John Lindley (1855), *The Theory and Practice of Horticulture; or, An Attempt to Explain The Chief Operations of Gardening upon Psychological Grounds* (Longman, Brown, Green and Longmans, London).

Charles Macintosh (1853), *The Book of the Garden*, 2 vols. (Blackwood, Edinburgh and London).

W. Robinson (1868), *Gleanings from French Gardens: Comprising an Account of Such Features of French Horticulture As Are Most Worthy of Adoption in British Gardens* (Frederick Warne, London).

—— (1871), *The Subtropical Garden; or, Beauty of Form in the Flower Garden* (John Murray, London).

——— (1881), *The Wild Garden; or the Naturalization and Natural Grouping of Hardy Exotic Plants with a Chapter on the Garden of British Wild Flowers* (John Murray, London).

——— (1883), *The English Flower Garden, Style, Position and Arrangement; followed by a Description, Alphabetically Arranged, of All the Plants Best Suited for its Embellishment; their Culture, and Positions suited for Each* (John Murray, London).

M.M. VILMORIN-ANDRIEUX (1885), *The Vegetable Garden: Illustrations, Descriptions, and Culture of the Garden Vegetables of Cold and Temperate Climates* (English edition published under the direction of W. Robinson), (John Murray, London).

Index

Page numbers in *italics* refer to captions for illustrations.
Page numbers in **bold** indicate recipes.

Picture Credits

All pictures copyright
Melanie Eclare except:

Every effort has been made to trace or contact all copyright holders. The publishers would be pleased to rectify any errors brought to their notice at the earliest opportunity.

Page 6 Courtesy Hugh Warne; **7** Courtesy Sylvia Davies; **8** (top) From M.M. Vilmorin-Andrieux, *The Vegetable Garden: Illustrations, Descriptions, and Culture of the Garden Vegetables of Cold and Temperate Climates;* (bottom) Courtesy the Lost Gardens of Heligan Archive; **9** Mary Evans Picture Library; **10–11** Courtesy the Lost Gardens of Heligan Archive; **12** Courtesy Pentewan Old Cornwall Society; **14** (top) From Macintosh, *Book of the Garden*, vol. 2; (bottom) Mary Evans Picture Library; **15** From Vilmorin-Andrieux, *The Vegetable Garden*; **17** Courtesy the Lost Gardens of Heligan Archive; **20** From Vilmorin-Andrieux, The Vegetable Garden; **24** From Macintosh, *Book of the Garden*, vol. 2; **26** From Macintosh, *Book of the Garden*, vol. 2; **29** From Macintosh, *Book of the Garden*, vol. 2; **31** From Vilmorin-Andrieux, The Vegetable Garden; **36** (top) From Vilmorin-Andrieux, *The Vegetable Garden*; (bottom) From Macintosh, *Book of the Garden*, vol. 2; **40** From Vilmorin-Andrieux, *The Vegetable Garden*; **42** From Vilmorin-Andrieux, *The Vegetable Garden*; **45** (top) From Vilmorin-Andrieux, *The Vegetable Garden*; (bottom) From Macintosh, *Book of the Garden*, vol. 2; **46** (bottom) From Macintosh, *Book of the Garden*, vol. 2; **49** From Vilmorin-Andrieux, *The Vegetable Garden*; **51–52** From Vilmorin-Andrieux, *The Vegetable Garden*; **54** (left) From Vilmorin-Andrieux, *The Vegetable Garden*; **55** From Vilmorin-Andrieux, The *Vegetable Garden*; **61** (bottom) From Vilmorin-Andrieux, *The Vegetable Garden*; **62** (right) From Vilmorin-Andrieux, *The Vegetable Garden*; **64** From Vilmorin-Andrieux, *The Vegetable Garden*; **73** From Vilmorin-Andrieux, *The Vegetable Garden*; **80–3** From Vilmorin-Andrieux, *The Vegetable Garden;* **90** (top) From Macintosh, *Book of the Garden*, vol. 2; **91** From Macintosh, *Book of the Garden*, vol. 2; **93** Jerry Harpur; **94** (top) From Macintosh, *Book of the Garden*, vol. 2; **96** From Macintosh, *Book of the Garden*, vol. 2; **98** From Jim Marter (ed), *Food and Drink: A Pictorial Archive from Nineteenth-Century Sources;* **100** (left) From Macintosh, *Book of the Garden*, vol. 2; **100** (right) From Macintosh, *Book of the Garden*, vol. 2; **101** Jerry Harpur; **103** From W.D. Drury (ed) *The Book Of Gardening;* **104** (top) From Vilmorin-Andrieux, *The Vegetable Garden;* **106** (bottom right) From Vilmorin-Andrieux, *The Vegetable Garden;* **107** Science Photo Library; **110** From Macintosh, *Book of the Garden*, vol. 2; **115** From Jim Marter (ed), *Food and Drink: A Pictorial Archive from Nineteenth-Century Sources;* **116** From William Forsyth *A Treatise on the Culture and Management of Fruit Trees;* **117** Jerry Harpur; **119** From Macintosh, *Book of the Garden*, vol. 2; **129** From Jim Marter (ed), *Food and Drink: A Pictorial Archive from Nineteenth-Century Sources;* **132** From Vilmorin-Andrieux, *The Vegetable Garden;* **134–135** Jerry Harpur; **148** (bottom) From W. Robinson, *The English Flower Garden;* **150–151** Jerry Harpur; **159** From Macintosh, *Book of the Garden*, vol. 2; **172** (top) From W. Robinson, *The Subtropical Garden;* **189** From W. Robinson *Gleanings from French Gardens*.

Acknowledgements

*It has been a great privilege to write a second book about Heligan. When I began
I thought it would never be possible but the thought of Melanie's exceptional photographs which would carry the text spurred me on. In fact writing about horticulture,
particularly the horticulture practised at Heligan, is very close to my heart. To be
able to follow on from* Heligan: A Portrait of the Lost Gardens *was a joy but to
concentrate heavily on the gardening techniques and the way it is done was a dream,
for I honestly believe that this place is like no other and the deeds and exploits of
the gardeners, past and present needed to be told.*

*The first person to thank is Candy Smit who, for the second time, has been
a huge help in so many ways. Likewise Peter Stafford, who allowed us to pester
the gardeners and just keep coming back and back.*

*Weidenfeld & Nicolson are fabulous publishers. Not only are they unbelievably
easy to work with but they also produce gorgeous books. Huge thanks to Michael
Dover for commissioning the book and keeping the ideas flowing and to David
Rowley for just getting the job done brilliantly and stylishly. Thanks also to Ken
Wilson for producing such a stunning book. Also to Jennie Condell who has stitched
the whole thing together and to Sue Webb who has somehow managed to clean up
my horrid, error strewn text.*

*I would like to thank Geoff Prettyman and the Pentewan Old Cornwall Society
for lending pictures for the book, that was kind and a big help Geoff, much appreciated.*

*But the real thanks must go to the gardeners, past and present, who made and
continue to make Heligan such an extraordinary place. We have taken up a lot of
your time in the last year but we really do appreciate it. So thanks to Sylvia, Helen,
Mike, Charles and Clive, to Annie and Haydn and to the Jungle crew, Mike and
Cindy. Mary and Trish, who keep the garden looking so lovely, thanks to you.
To Jim, Tony and Matt who climbed trees for us and to Adrian, Dave and Bob for
their understanding too — holding heavy stuff while the camera clicked away. Thanks
to Andy and Irv for a little slice of sanity every now and then and thanks to everone
in the office for trying to connect me to Sheperd's Barn. Thank you to the garden
for giving up her secrets but thanks most of all to my darling Melanie for your
amazing photographs.*

First published in Great Britain in 2006
by Weidenfeld & Nicolson

10 9 8 7 6 5 4 3 2 1

Text copyright © Tom Petherick 2006
Pictures copyright © Melanie Eclare, except
as indicated on page 207.
Design and layout © Weidenfeld & Nicolson
2006

All rights reserved. No part of this publication
may be reproduced, stored in a retrieval
system, or transmitted, in any form or by any
means, electronic, mechanical, photocopying,
recording or otherwise, without the prior
permission of both the copyright owner and
the above publisher.

The right of the copyright holders to be
identified as the authors of this work has been
asserted in accordance with the Copyright,
Designs and Patents Act 1988.

A CIP catalogue record for this book is available
from the British Library.

ISBN-13: 978 0 297 84405 1
ISBN-10: 0 297 84405 9

Printed and bound in Italy

Design director: David Rowley
Designed by Ken Wilson
Colour reproduction by DL Interactive
Editor: Jennie Condell
Editorial by Sue Webb and Rosie Anderson
Index by Chris Bell
Research by Brónagh Woods

Weidenfeld & Nicolson
The Orion Publishing Group Ltd
Wellington House
125 Strand
London, WC2R 0BB

The Orion Publishing Group's policy is to
use papers that are natural, renewable and
recyclable products and made from wood
grown in sustainable forests. The logging
and manufacturing processes are expected
to conform to the environmental regulations
of the country of origin.

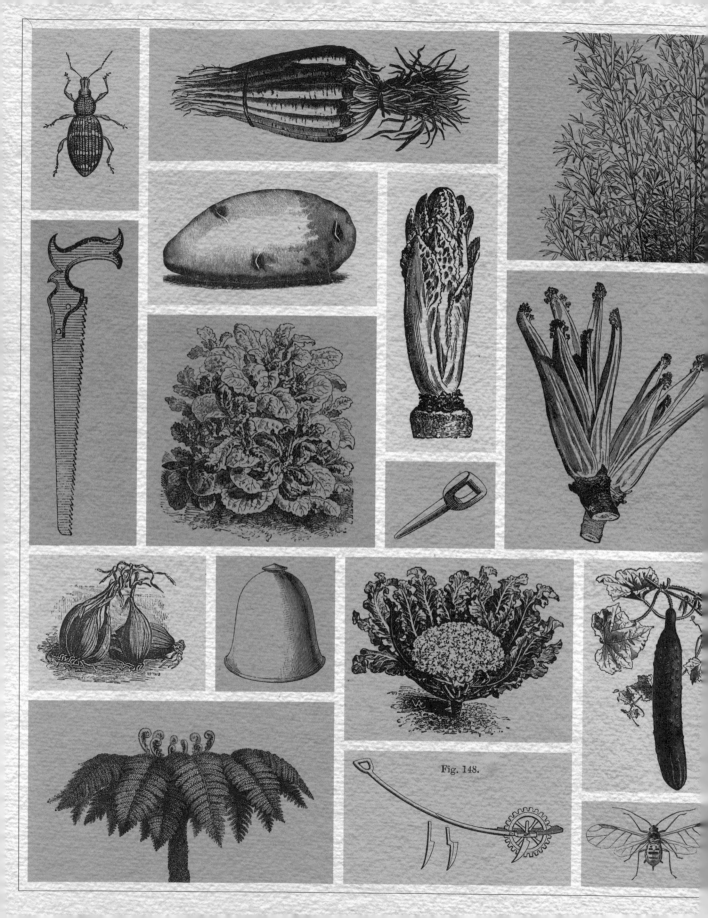

Fig. 148.